MOTHERHOOD, MOTHER SHOULD

Kathleen Brown

Motherhood, Mother Should

Copyright ©2021 Kathleen Brown

ISBN   979-8-9851375-0-7   Hardcover
ISBN   979-8-9851375-1-4   Paperback
ISBN   979-8-9851375-2-1   eBook

LCCN 2021922599

Edited by Jenny Margotta
Book design by StoriesToTellBooks.com

Dedication

To all those who raise children to make this world a better place.

Special Thanks to My Mom - Barbara Campfield
Marcus Petitt - written collaboration
Melanie Conley - written collaboration
Makiah Green - written collaboration

CONTENTS

Part II Teaching the Four Cornerstones of Success

Part III Pace and Push

Part IV The Empowerment of Mom

Left: Solange Brown, Licensed Vocational Nurse. Right: Christopher Brown, Registered Nurse, Wound Care Specialist.

Matthew Brown, Doctor of Dental Surgery and Nicholas Brown, Doctor of Chiropractic Medicine.

Dr. Michelle Brown, Doctor of Dental Surgery.

Kenneth D. Brown, non-profit management.

Melanie Lasseigne, Psychiatrist Mental Health Nurse Practitioner.

PREFACE

Children are a wonderful addition to our lives. They are our seeds, our legacy, our challenge, the extension of ourselves.

Don't think that you have already won your race. What is needed is to always improve, forget what is behind, and do your best to reach for what is ahead. So run straight toward the goal in order to win the prize of your race.

Over the years many people have asked my husband and me about our big family. They ask us how we were able to raise a large family in this day with its many diversions, challenges, and obstacles. They are astounded by the way each of our seven children—Solange, Kenneth, Melanie, Chris, Michelle, Matthew and Nicholas, who are all now adults—have completed or are completing college or post-graduate education, four on full, four-year scholarships and two just shy of full scholarships. The Internal Revenue Service even audited us one year because our finances were questioned. There was doubt that one family could support five children attending 3 four-year universities at the same time and have Mom in college as well. After submitting all of their scholarship information, birth certificates, and years of medical records, the IRS agent released us, baffled yet astonished. Still others wonder at how all of our kids seem directed and are working toward professional goals or aspirations. They are amazed that our children seem to be genuinely kindhearted people.

Those looking in from the outside inquisitively ask us questions ranging from, "How did you afford the cost of raising a large family in a major metropolitan city in these trying times?" to "How did you feed everyone? What did you cook for dinner every night?" Well, as our family has evolved, the answers have varied, depending on the numerous phases and events circulating around our home. The constant challenges my husband and I witnessed were comparable to running an obstacle course that changed as we maneuvered through it. Undeniably, I can honestly answer that there have been many up and down moments.

People even have the nerve to ask us why we had so many children. I can usually reply that, despite medical prevention and my husband's vasectomy, I guess you better ask the Good Lord. Yes, the twins came after my husband was snipped. Despite our unusual situation, God has blessed us by enabling us to adjust and adapt when necessary.

Modern family balance is impacted by societal demands and pressures that previous generations did not face. This is compounded with the accessibility to media, which molds our social expectations by exploiting the shock factor. In addition, our children are being exposed to things like brutality and self-gratification before they are able to discern right from wrong. Without guidance, young minds are pushed and pulled away from actions that promote a strong foundation. As a team, my husband and I have tried our best to keep our children focused on the right path by instilling in them strong values and a plan of direction. Physical and mental challenges, sacrifices, and the implementation of discipline and expectations have all been obstacles in our parental race.

Motherhood, Mother Should focuses on the day-to-day stride of our family's race. Yes, Mom, not only do you deal with your own personal race, but each member of your family also has his/her own purpose, and each is like a relay team member that depends upon one another to push the team forward. And Mom, you are the coach, the organizer, the trainer, the disciplinarian and the cheerleader that drives that energy. If you are a good coach, then your team will produce. If you are a single mom, or a grandparent raising children for the second time, then your role as a mentor is even more important as you and your family keep pace.

I hope my experiences and parental advice will assist those who feel apprehensive, confused, or overwhelmed by the immense challenges of motherhood. Advice is cheap, but knowledge and experience are powerful. If anything I write helps to answer an unsolved problem or gain the calmness of introspection, then I have continued to be a mother to others as well.

Sometimes, your parental path is and will be a grind. Sometimes, you might miss your freedom and desire to return to how life was before you had kids. At times things will get intense, with many victories and many failures, and you will shed tears, but, Mom, keep your head up. You must realize that life is meant to have the unpredictability of children. The cookie-cutter life of couples who have chosen to have a pet rather than children may bring about a life that is orderly, but kids bring a challenge that makes life more interesting, as each child is different and complex. The specialty of motherhood is a unique responsibility which brings into being that special blessing that only your child will become.

As our family has run our race together, my children have taught me just as much as I have taught them. In doing for them, they have taught me calmness, confidence, and patience. I have learned to better myself and evolve as a person through the challenges that my husband and I have faced.

My book is divided into four sections:

Part I: Lessen the Lesson, is devoted to the way in which you as a mom show your child the positive pathways through life by the use of example, mentoring, and spoken expectations.

Part II: Teaching the Four Cornerstones of Success, describes the four things you need to teach your children to help them gain a successful life.

Part III: Pace and Push focuses on the daily schedule our family followed and the sequential path of each of our children from childhood to young adulthood which resulted in their scholarships and present achievements.

Part IV: The Empowerment of Mom focuses on the daily practice to help balance your personal life with motherhood and to make your job more manageable so you can achieve with your family as a team as you win your race together.

PART I

LESSEN THE LESSON

Our kids playing on the swing set in the yard.

Chapter 1

Be a Great Mom, Not a Perfect Mom

*Happy is anyone who becomes wise, who comes to
have understanding*

~Proverbs 3:13

It is impossible to be perfect, let alone be a perfect parent. No one has ever been perfect, because we are all human. Perfection is a human thought, so you can be assured there is no such thing. There are many messages that seep into our brain about what a perfect mom should be doing to raise perfect children. Unfortunately, the "perfect mom superhuman" does not exist. I will be the first to admit that I am not a perfect mom, but the good news is that great moms do exist—and you are on your path to becoming a *great mom*!

The realities of everyday life impact us all. No matter how much experience we have, there is no optimal way to handle every turn of your child's younger years. The independent variables of place, time, situation, family culture, and your child's personality make motherhood the ultimate "think on your feet" job.

I remember one Sunday when we had to get ready for our usual 10:00 church service. We had to get everyone up at 6:30, including our youngest, the twins, who were infants. Getting seven youngsters from ages eleven down to two months fully dressed and ready was always an adventure, yet we did our best to set a Sunday morning routine each week. Every morning was always a rush and this Sunday was no different. After nursing both twins, fixing breakfast for nine, ironing, and directing the older children to help the younger ones get dressed, we headed out to our station wagon by 9:30 for a simple, five-minute drive. We looked like the characters in the vacation departure scene from "Home Alone," constantly running and bumping into each other. Loading the station wagon, diaper bag in tow, we checked our seatbelts, "Check," double-checked the car's head count, "Check, check," and then off we drove. As usual, we arrived several minutes late, and our long line of children filed into the empty pew that was gracefully saved for us each week by fellow church members.

This particular Sunday I felt a sense of pride as we all sat down looking clean, tidy, and Godly. I could finally take a deep breath. As I scanned the pew, eager to view my perfect, Godly-looking children, I saw Michelle, my two-year-old daughter, sitting spread legged with no underpants on. Trying to look cool, I hoisted both Michelle and Christopher, who was then four, and headed to the church bathroom, where I quickly transferred his Spiderman underwear onto his sister. My son, now "underwearless," looked at me oddly as I buttoned his church pants and walked right back to the pew. No one else noticed my inward panic or what had happened, except for Chris and Michelle, of course.

My personal slip-ups on this and other occasions are an assurance that there is no such thing as a perfect mom.

I probably was the worst tooth fairy ever. One of my disappointed, teary-eyed children would often come to me with a bloody tooth in hand, asking, "Why did the tooth fairy forget me again?" Needless to say, I fell short time and time again of that hypothetical but highly coveted "Perfect Mom Prize."

It is so important for you to understand that although you are not a perfect mom, you have everything it takes to be a great mom! If you have a good heart, and consistently give your best effort by using your head, your wits, and thinking outside the box for the sake of your children, then you are what I would consider to be an awesome mom! I think I eventually became a "great" mom because I started recognizing my mistakes as a way to improve my mothering skills.

There is a scripture, 2 Corinthians 12:9, which states that when a person is weak, or weakened, they are able to learn from their mistakes and become stronger. The more one learns from life's lessons, the wiser they become. Though I fondly think back to that church underwear experience, it was not the end of the world, but I learned that I should have been more prepared by packing my diaper bag the night before to save time and pack an emergency pair of underwear for each of my kids under the age of eight. Even so, I was proud of myself for thinking creatively to solve the problem at hand.

Anticipation of potential kid problems is developed through lessons learned, commonsense, and trial and error. A great mom is not born or developed by classes or books. That is why motherhood is so exciting and challenging. Your experience will be totally different than any other mommy and your child's experience with you will be a unique one. You have what you need inside of you, so begin with baby steps as a mom before you begin to run. Your best teacher is experience, so if you make a mistake, keep running, but always take your kids with you on the path of your race.

KNOW YOUR CHILDREN'S PERSONALITIES

As you guide your children, you learn to know each child's character, unique ways, temperaments, and idiosyncrasies. Solange, our oldest, was the most independent of all our children. A natural performer, she was a talkative and extremely outgoing child. She has a comical, actress personality with a quick wit and has always found a way to perform in front of others. She memorized every line of dialog from "The Little Mermaid" and would sing the film score upon request.

As my first child, I wanted to expose her to everything I felt would direct her toward a bright future as a doctor or lawyer. Yet, as she grew, I realized that my role was to help her experience the things that would direct her to find her own desired path. My job was to give her support in her interests, in whatever direction she chose. She already had the necessary confidence to guide herself toward what she needed to accomplish.

Kenneth was the quiet and thoughtful one around others, yet he could be silly and goofy if he knew you well. He was very methodical in everything he did and had a great tenacity toward his interests. He loved small plastic army figures and always had a makeshift fort formed from blankets and a wobbly card table in the living room. To help his shyness, we always pushed him to do the things he did well. Hands-on projects and sports were how we directed him to bloom and accomplish his goals. He had to declare his ground, especially since he was sandwiched between his two sisters, Solange, who is two years older, and Melanie, who is nineteen months younger.

Melanie was affectionately called "Little Grandma" because she was the smallest of the kids and into everyone's business. Her amiable personality and bright smile welcomed everyone into her situations. She always had a collection of dolls in carriages dragging behind her, and she loved to sing Whitney Houston songs in the mirror. She concerned me the most because she had such an easy-going, "low maintenance," vulnerable personality. I worried that she might be too kind to others at times. She never gave me any problems, so she was always under the radar in comparison to her six siblings. Being the middle child of seven is tough, so we pushed her with competitive activities such as tennis and academics as she got into higher grades.

Christopher was known as "Tornado Boy" because of his high energy and activity level. He was constantly flying from our couch to the floor with a superhero cape made from a dishtowel tied around his neck. He was always in imagination mode, saving the world from evil villains. Riding on his Big Wheel bike twenty times a day across the living room floor was typical for him. He, like his dad, was always on an entrepreneurial quest. He was competitive. As a three-year-old, Chris made money by selling preschool projects he made in class to whoever would buy them for a minimum of $2.00. On the back of his big wheel, bags of glued, wooden totem poles and other holiday creations would be towed to close neighbors' homes or kindly panhandled to visiting family members or friends. Everyone always knew to save an extra buck or two for Christopher. His teacher once told me that she had never seen a student turn preschool into a business.

Chris needed boundaries because he had an active nature. He needed to know his limits, but we also encouraged his need to extend his hands-on competitiveness. We pushed him by wisely creating opportunities that helped him focus and channel his energy in a positive way.

Michelle, our fifth child, was our most challenging. She was tough-minded and the most demanding of all our children. She was the one who challenged our patience, as she required the most attention and consistently questioned authority. She and Solange always developed eczema—a skin rash—during the warmer months, so when they were irritable, they milked sympathy as a way to get attention from the others. Daily tantrums would result as Michelle had to compete with her twin infant brothers, Nicholas and Matthew, also who took up a lot of our attention. She was the smartest and most competitive; she took care of herself academically, taking top honors every year. To handle her constant success, we had to correct her shrewd personality. She had to be included in every family activity so she would become more aware of her siblings and sensitive to others.

The twins always had fun together. They were each other's best friend and managed to ignore problems around them by keeping occupied with one another. They could turn a simple chore into a wrestling match on the floor at any time, day or night. They were the last of the kids, and I guess they were babied a little more than the others. They were competitive with each other and often so playful that they would lose focus on being serious when necessary. I guess "happy go lucky" would be a good term to describe them, so we needed to encourage better schoolwork ethic at home while communicating with teachers and keep a ceiling on their playfulness while pushing them both in a good direction to foster their individual personalities.

Lessons Learned on the Go

Mothers must learn through experience. When you know your child and evaluate his or her experiences, you learn how to handle each situation and each child differently. You begin to develop problem-solving skills as you both journey through the race of life's many surprises. By navigating through trial-and-error situations, you develop that eighth sense of motherhood problem solving. These experiences come as you take your child with you into the big world as often as possible. Taking your young child around town also helps you truly experience motherhood, as you are newly exposed to the constant demands of commonsense training. Visits to the store, the park, or church help your baby or young child learn about the world and train them how to act outside the home.

We all have so much to do, and little ones can slow down your pace. Yet outings are a great way for you and your child to spend time together and learn about the world, even if it is at the end of a long and tiring day. I will be the first to admit that I took advantage whenever a neighbor or family member volunteered to watch my younger toddlers while I ran out for a quick trip to the store. But when possible, take your children with you so they can learn from you in various settings. To make the trip easier, here are some tips to employ before going on an errand:

1. The day before your trip, write a list of where you need to go and what you need to buy at each place.

2. Prepare your bag and place it by the door the day before any outing. Pin a list of diaper bag necessities inside your bag so you have what you need—such as extra underpants. (Hee-hee.)

3. Always plan your errands, but always go to the farthest destination first. This will save you both time and gas, helping to make errand time quicker. Remember the old Boy Scout model, "Be prepared." It can save you a lot of backtracking.

4. Talk to your children while you are traveling. Keep them involved in the trip by asking questions, pointing to places of interest, and explaining where and why you are going on the errand. In other words, keep them involved so they can join in with you on your adventure and not tune you out. But more importantly, learn from your daily lessons dealing with your child. Be aware of how much "tolerance time" your child can endure. A two-hour trip might be good for your child, but extending the trip to three or four hours might result in a tired baby or a cranky toddler and a lower patience level for Mom.

5. Always have your kids use the potty before they go on a two- or three-hour outing. This will lessen the need for stops and eliminate the hassle of finding a clean bathroom, which can be very difficult.

6. Take a pair of pajamas with you so that, on those long days or evening field trips, you can change your children in the car and, when you get home, you can slip them right into bed without having to undress them first.

As you go through life's routines, things will come up. Decisions made in a grocery aisle, such as deciding which diaper brand to use, may take longer than expected, but remember to pace your outings wisely to avoid antsy babies and children. Try to move at a good pace to avoid the negative behaviors that arise from boredom. Don't forget that your children are watching you and learning how to act in public. From what you buy to how you interact with others, they are soaking everything in. Through your everyday actions, you are teaching your child how to cope, make decisions, and communicate with others, among other basic skills they will need throughout their lives. Although there are certain advantages to letting your child stay at home, the real world experiences they receive from leaving the house are invaluable.

DISCERNING—HOW TO BE A GREAT MOM!

> *You must follow the example of good people.*
> *Pay attention and you will have wisdom.*
> —Proverbs 4:1

In addition to learning from your mistakes, observing other moms and discerning good advice from simple wives' tales is an essential way to gain wisdom. I give credit to my own mom, who taught me as she modeled dignity and stern behavior to make our home function. Many things I did as a mom came from watching my mom, yet everyone's experience is dependent upon individual circumstances.

As a track enthusiast, I know that a runner's mind can make or break a race. You stand at the starting line, excited and ready to go as you check out your competition. Your mind begins to play games with you as you see younger, sculptured physiques ready to compete. You begin to doubt yourself and your ability to win. The mind plays games, causing intimidation, and, later, affects your performance, especially if you are an inexperienced runner.

First-time mothers often feel like the inexperienced runner at the starting line. As a new mom you start with an enthusiastic desire to be a perfect mom to your newborn. You go through nine months of pregnancy, hoping that every doctor's appointment leads to a beautiful and perfect bundle. You try to do everything right by taking your vitamins, exercising, and reading books to your womb, hoping to develop that future Einstein. Then, after the baby comes, you enter the unfamiliar territory of trial and error as you embark on your journey of raising this helpless little person.

Sometimes, it is the mother who is more helpless. I recall that I had absolutely no experience with babies before my firstborn, Solange. Unfortunately, there were no young mothers in our close family or friend group for me to observe. Also, I lacked experience because I didn't have younger siblings with which to practice Baby-101 strategies. On my first night in the hospital, I was in pain and exhausted from twenty-two hours of labor. Fred was in the cafeteria when the nurse brought in our baby from the nursery to spend the first night. She was beautiful and tiny. The moment was great as I held this little life for the first time.

Once the nurse left, I heard what sounded like a little, muffled toot, and I knew exactly what it meant: her first poop. I had to pull my feelings of incompetence together and put my child first. I dove in and untied my neat, tightly swaddled child, trying to remember the folding pattern so I could rewrap her the same way. Once I wiped her clean, I reached for a clean diaper, but then more poop kept flowing out again and again. While holding her head, I began to feel tense as the brown mess spread past the containment of the diaper, onto the hospital bedding, and, eventually, upon me.

Just then a large nurse with a thick accent entered the room, patiently scolding me on what I should be doing. Another nurse came in, and they both saw that I had crashed and burned on my first attempt to change a diaper. They chuckled as they spoke in their native language. I felt embarrassed, but I knew this would be the first of many tries. Although I had stumbled out the starting gate, I was, like my newborn, experiencing something new for the first time.

Infancy to Toddler Stage
(Newborn to Age Two)

My first days were awkward and often messy as poop and breast milk flowed everywhere. I experienced a lack of sleep due to Solange waking up and crying because she had colic, which is a large amount of gas in the stomach or intestines. It's a common infant condition that causes discomfort and irritability. She always had difficulty sleeping at night between 3 and 6 a.m. Being full of gas also hindered her from taking sufficient naps during the day because her stomach was full with air, especially after a meal.

Most mothers use naptime to either rest themselves or get something done. With Solange not napping during the day and then being up at night, I felt tired, and I needed help. There were people constantly coming by, and I desperately sought advice from more-experienced mothers. At first I thought it was great having the first baby in the immediate generation of my family, because everyone was more than willing to give advice. But eventually, an interesting pressure arose, as everyone believed their advice was the best. I learned fifteen different ways to address the needs of a colicky baby, from drinking peppermint tea two hours before nursing to blowing cigarette smoke up my baby's rectum.

Finally, I took the best advice from my grandmother, JJ, who told me to watch my diet because something I was eating was probably causing Solange to have gas after nursing. She told me to avoid eating chocolate, onions, or spicy foods. After trying this out, I realized she was right. It is good to talk to experienced moms because they have a wealth of wisdom and anecdotes to comfort you as they relive their own baby-battle stories. But it's imperative to be selective and choose the solutions that will fit your specific situation.

Remember, each baby is different. Be flexible and understand that what works for one baby doesn't always work for another. As a young mom, choose, watch, and learn from other great moms. Too much advice may confuse you, but it is important to listen, ask plenty of questions, and discern the best plan through logic and trial and error.

As a mom of seven, I have my own advice for new moms:

1. Breastfeeding is the most beneficial way to feed and nourish your baby. Breast milk is rich in fat and helps promote a good immune system to protect your infant's health. It may hurt at first, and you will need patience as both you and your baby learn together during this special time. It may be difficult as well, especially if you are a working mom, but taking an automatic pump to work may help alleviate some of the pressure. Automatic pumps can be purchased from organizations like the La Leche League. Try to nurse for six months to a year. Some mothers choose to breastfeed and use bottled formula for convenience, especially if they work. Nursing or bottle-feeding your baby in a quiet place is imperative because this time is important for bonding and developing love for each other. You may choose to pump at work, then nurse at home after things settle down in the evenings. If you are only formula bottle-feeding, the same holds true. Quiet time with your baby is essential, so go into your room, away from others, turn off the TV and the cell phone, and try your best to have "Mommy time" in a calm place.

2. Sleep deprivation is a reality for most parents with newborns. It is common to want to do something that makes your baby sleep better, but never sleep next to your infant

in bed. Although sleepless nights might make lying down while nursing or bottle-feeding very tempting, you might roll over onto your baby and accidently smother them. In the event your baby starts choking, you would be completely unaware. Also, do not lay your infant on their stomach, especially at night. This will reduce the chance of crib death (Sudden Infant Death Syndrome), which can occur in newborns under three months. Remember to always consult your physician on all medical advice.

3. Do not bathe your baby every night to encourage relaxation. Babies do not get that dirty, and you will just dry out their skin. A soothing massage as part of your bedtime routine will calm and help your baby to sleep better. Lastly, babies seem to sleep better if there is a droning noise or white noise to listen to as they sleep. I do not know why this occurs, but just like when you are driving in a car with your baby, noise or a soothing vibration lulls them to "La-La Land" almost every time. Some moms turn on the dryer or vacuum cleaner. Some monitors have soft music that seems to work just as well.

4. Hold your baby as often as you can. Babies need love and touch to develop a sense of comfort and interaction.

5. Spend as much time as possible with your baby during the first year. Do not simply watch your child; incorporate physical and emotional interaction such as playing, reading, singing, and looking at your baby's face to encourage bonding. You are probably wondering where you find the time for this. Well, busy moms can't create time, but we can maximize it by prioritizing what we do with our time. Everyone is given twenty-four hours in each day. How you

spend that time as a new mom can give you more time than you think to be with your child.

6. Control your finances. If you anticipate pregnancy or if you are pregnant, make an effort to maintain a responsible budget and spend within your means to avoid too much debt. The more debt you have, the more you must work to pay bills, which subtracts time from being with your baby. If you have earned vacation days, they can be scheduled to extend your maternity leave. Babies need direct love from their parents more than they need the latest shoes or fancy clothes. Working late or juggling two jobs so your family can have the latest electronics or fashions will use up precious time that could be spent with your child.

7. Simplify your household expenses. Although this is tough to do, it *can* be done. When I had my daughter Solange, I was a twenty-two-year-old secretary and decided to stay home for the first three years of rearing. I knew that going to work could and would be expensive, as you must pay for childcare, work clothes, and gas to commute. Instead, I planned to stay home and work part time at home doing odd jobs, such as typing college papers for students or babysitting other children. I cut my expenses by breastfeeding rather than buying formula, trading hand-me-downs with extended family, and making baby food in my blender. I also cooked dinner at home and made my husband's lunch daily. I know in this economy it is required that one or both parents work, go to school, or both, but if you can budget wisely, you can do it. Many mothers are running small businesses at home through the internet or bartering services to others. If both parents work or are in school, try to develop a schedule that allows your baby to

have quality time with at least one parent for several hours every day. If you need a babysitter, use a trusted family member or a well-recommended caregiver until you can take over after work. Although you will be exhausted most nights—we know this, Mom—dig deep and know that your baby's cry mean that he or she really needs something. Sit down, put the baby on your chest, and love on them. Believe it or not, the time will relax both of you.

8. If at times the house looks like a wreck, and it will, do not worry; in most cases, housework can be caught up later. Develop a support system and find others to assist you with dinner and cleaning. During my most intense times, I used my slow cooker at least four times a week. I would cut up vegetables, chicken or beef, beans, etc. in the morning before work, and it would be finished when I got home around 6 p.m. Your baby's first year will go quickly, and you shouldn't miss it by obsessing over chores.

9. I recommend that you don't feed your baby solid foods until they are six months old. Even though you desire to sleep more, introducing solids could result in allergies or possible weight problems due to a baby's immature digestion system that is still unable to digest solids. Remember, consult your physician for medical advice.

Now that I have put in my two cents, you must tweak this advice and apply it to your own life. Your child and your situation are different from mine, so be creative, listen to experienced moms, allocate, and think on your feet for your baby's wellbeing as well as your own. Keep a small journal to remember what worked and what did not work so that the first few months with your second child will be a little easier.

CREATE GOOD MODELING—THE COPYCAT YEARS (AGES TWO THROUGH FIVE)

I call ages two through five the Copycat Stage because your child looks at you and learns how to act in every situation. They want to be like you, so they imitate you. I have had the pleasure of reuniting with parents of former school acquaintances of my parents who have stated how I remind them of my mom or dad when they were young. From my dad, who was a teacher, I inherited my love of performing lessons in front of students. He loved to study and digested facts from history books and periodicals. From him I have also inherited the art of eating too fast. From my mom I inherited the tough-minded personality from her southern, Louisiana roots.

My mother's family lived during the Depression and times of segregation, so they are proud, but they are also hot tempered at times. As a child I witnessed the bad temper of my maternal grandfather as he put his fist through the car windshield after the radio announced that a baseball batter had struck out during a Dodger game. I know that I have acquired a short temper because it was a norm in my household as I was growing up.

Subliminally, you react just like your mentors show you how to react. You have to fight these urges of emotions in front of your children because children absorb the behavior they observe. Whether good or bad, your actions influence your child's personality.

ALWAYS TAKE TIME TO MODEL SAFETY

No matter how busy you are, always make time to ensure your child is safe. Things can happen so fast. Children ages two through five investigate and copy everything, so be prepared for their curiosity. Taking the time to be precautious for your baby or child is time well spent to avoid potential harm. No matter how much of a rush you are in, take time for the following safety measures:

1. Fasten your car seat properly. Take your car and the car seat to your local police department to ensure size compliance and that the straps are positioned correctly.

2. Safeguard your home. There are many websites that can assist you with ideas and solutions. Safeguard your crib by assembling it correctly with bolts securely tightened so your baby does not squirm into tight places that could choke or smother. Make sure there are no drape chords hanging around the crib. These can constrict your baby's throat or even hang the child.

3. Secure all cabinets so that dangerous items, such as bleach and poisons, are not in your child's reach.

4. Put hazardous materials away as soon as possible. At three years old, my son Kenneth ate a fistful of pink orchid fertilizer after I left it on the floor as I went to answer the phone. It only took a few seconds for me to answer the phone, take a message, and return to see my son with pink drool dripping from his mouth. The poison control operator chuckled as she assured me he had simply eaten fancy cow poop and that everything would be okay. Although it seems like a funny story to share in retrospect, I was frightened and worried out of my mind at the moment. As your children get older, the risks are not as comical.

5. Make a head count before going somewhere or leaving an event. Small children are inquisitive and tend to wander off. Hold your child by the hand in large crowds, and do not be preoccupied with other activities. I have seen parents scroll through their cell phone messages while walking in front of their toddler, assuming the child is strolling behind them. Pay attention to your children, because they are your

first priority. You can answer a text or return a call later. Distractions at a park or event can unfortunately open the door for predators looking for a wandering child.

6. Be aware of pets around young infants and toddlers. Pets can be unpredictable, as they must now share their owner's love and attention. So please, never, never leave your child alone with your pet, especially if the pet has been in your household for a while. Jealousy may occur.

7. Make an inventory of all potential problem areas in your house. Create a contingency plan in case of emergencies and share it with your family. Your children will benefit from your model of safety and will develop a sense of vigilance and responsibility.

Chapter 2

Rearing Your Child
toward Good Behavior
by Fostering Outer and Inner Discipline

Every aspect of life requires discipline, from a runner who needs to train to the fledging bird learning to fly. Without discipline there is no progression toward betterment. The Webster dictionary contains two definitions of discipline. The first is: *Training or conditioning imposed for the improvement of physical power or self-control.*

I will go a little further and expound on two kinds of discipline: outer and inner discipline. I know that when I drive I need to exhibit certain behaviors, such as stopping at a red light. I have been trained by outside forces to stop so that I will not have the negative consequence of harming myself in an accident or receiving a hefty ticket. I call this outer discipline. In similar fashion, adults have the responsibility of teaching children how to operate in the world around them; namely, at school, in the store, on a sports team, anywhere. We must establish the boundaries of behavior for our children to protect them physically and help them to become socially acceptable.

Webster also defines discipline as: *the training that corrects, molds, or perfects mental faculties.* I call this inner discipline, which is a person's inner drive—the self-learning of rules or codes toward a desired outcome. As we mature we want to learn new skills or challenge our abilities to go further in life, such as completing a degree or just sticking to a diet. The first type of discipline impacts and overlaps the second, which is manifested on a daily basis.

OUTER DISCIPLINE
(NEWBORN TO AGE TWO)

1. Teaching outer discipline is important when physical boundaries require rules for protection and safety. Environmental hazards such as electrical appliances, caustic items, and fragile valuables within a house should not be touched and must be considered off limits. As your baby begins to crawl and walk, behavior boundaries must be determined, and learning cause and effect needs to be consistently applied. Learning outer discipline begins with learning the word "no."

   Parents, using the word "no" as soon as your child learns to crawl is essential. Even as young as five months, babies start to realize that certain things are not to be touched.

2. Be consistent with your "no." If your child wants something and "no" is an inconsistent reply, they will find flexibility and gaps in your discipline rules. They will keep trying to get around your rules, hoping to eventually wear you out with constant whining, nagging, or tantrums.

3. Explain why you said no. This will help your child understand why the addressed item is off limits. Many parents pull their child away from danger but do not explain the reason for the correction. A child will usually try again out of curiosity, but stand firm and understand that saying "no" is for their greater good, no matter how much they protest. Share the same rules with the other adults or siblings in the house so the child understands that the rule is universal.

4. Positive reinforcement will assure that good behavior continues. Always praise your child when they do something that is pleasing to you. Hugs and kisses should always be in abundance when something is done well. Balance love and discipline, lest there be too many rules and not enough pleasure. The most successful disciplinarians are firm in both correction and personal affirmation.

As a mom, I made an effort to never give my child power over my decisions, my schedule, or me. We always confined our errands to a two-hour maximum because it seemed tolerable for both sides. As mentioned before, limit long errands. Two-hour trips are more bearable when your child knows the destinations and the reason for each stop before you reach it.

If a trip went longer than expected, I would sometimes—but not often—buy my children ice cream or a treat for good behavior. I never informed them of the treat prior to getting it, so they did not believe they were entitled to tangible rewards as a result of expected behavior. Since they never knew when to expect it, it kept them on their toes.

EARLY CHILDHOOD AND OUTER DISCIPLINE (AGES TWO TO SIX)

As a child reaches the toddler stage, they are able to walk to things, reach for things, and use limited requests. (i.e. "Mommy, I want cookie.") This is the best time to teach them how to obey your rules. If you are consistent with your rules, your child will respond to you with more respect.

1. State your rules clearly. When your child is able to repeat a rule, have them repeat it after you.

2. Develop consequences and rewards for your child—this is where we as parents tend to be the most confused. What is the best punishment? How often should I employ it? And how much is enough? As a mom, I have a hierarchy of behaviors that result in different consequences or rewards. Before punishing, though, you must understand the situation so you better understand why your child is behaving a certain way. Was the behavior used to get attention? Is your child lacking in something that is causing discomfort? Are they hungry, cold, or frustrated? Many parents want to react before asking these questions, but this is not always fair. Even as a teacher, before doling out a punishment, I listened to the situation or circumstance first from all parties involved.

LISTENING VERSUS REACTING IS IMPERATIVE

One example of listening before reacting occurred when my twins were very young. This became one of my most memorable events of my children growing up. I had just dropped off my kids at school. My twins, who were about eighteen months old at the time, were snuggled in their car seats. The morning was foggy and mist was falling on my windshield. I pulled into our yard and began my usual routine of taking the twins out of the car and putting them into their cribs. I took Nicholas out of the car and put him on the sofa to change him. As I was unwrapping him, I heard our clothes dryer buzz loudly. I realized that Matthew must have climbed out of his crib and made his way to the back porch to push the dryer button—the one thing he had learned over the weekend and was now doing over and over again.

On the fourth or fifth buzz, I called out to Matthew to stop, but the buzzing continued. As I finished with Nicholas, I started walking toward the back porch. As I entered the kitchen, I heard the dryer door slam close and then heard a muffled SHREEK from our cat. I ran to the dryer as Matthew was still pushing the button and realized that the scream was coming from inside the dryer. I opened the door and the cat leaped from his imprisonment to make a mad dash out our kitchen, through the living room, and out the hole in our front door screen. Matthew had put the cat in the dryer and was attempting to turn it on with the cat still inside. Luckily, he had not closed the door of the dryer when I was changing Nicholas or the machine would have started and the cat would have been a bag of bones.

I looked at Matthew with an upset face. He was startled as he looked back at me. I raised my voice and said, "Matthew, how could you do this, you could have killed the cat. What were you thinking?"

His eyes filled up with big tears as he said, "Cat, cat wet."

At this point Nicholas came running to see what all the commotion was about. At that moment I realized that our cat, which lives in our yard, had become damp from the morning fog. Apparently, Matthew had wanted to help the cat by drying him in the clothes dryer. It made perfect sense to a toddler. He had seen me take wet clothes and put them into this magic machine that would turn them into nice, hot, fluffy clothes. I looked at him and realized that I could not be mad. He was trying to help the cat, not kill it. With tears quietly flowing, I gave him a big hug and told him to use a towel the next time.

Situations like this happen all the time. Our children may do something that makes perfect sense to them at the time. But before jumping to conclusions and punishments, investigate the situation by asking what happened. Breathe and take a minute to decide the proper outcome for the situation. Depending on the behavior and the level of action, I used a protocol of punishment.

OUTER DISCIPLINE PUNISHMENT PROTOCOL FOR EARLY CHILDHOOD (AGES TWO THROUGH ELEVEN)

Level I. Curiosity is a natural part of a child's learning process. Young children learn through hands-on investigation. As parents we must shape their curiosity while simultaneously helping them to avoid danger. When my son Chris was a toddler, he was very active. In one instance he took an interest in electrical outlets and began walking toward one—to investigate it, of course. He understood that outlets were off limits and I was not playing.

You will probably say "no" twenty times a day to a sixteen-month-old child, but this sets the limits. Make sure to say the word "no" clearly and firmly. You may also state, "No Touch." This simple command helps children understand that you are the one in power. Non-compliance to the word "no" may lead to the next level of discipline.

Level II. This punishment level consists of taking the child's pleasure away without an argument or power struggle. For me, this level usually involved my child ignoring a command, not sharing with a sibling, whining, or refusing to complete a task.

When Solange and Kenneth were young, I encouraged them to "share play." Kenneth had little plastic army men that he loved to play with but would only share with his sister on occasion. Sometimes, he wanted to play by himself, which was fine, but at other times he would notice his sister playing with his toys, rush over, and take them away from her. I would tell him, "Kenneth, must share. Your sister always shares with you." In most cases, this compelled him to comply, but on some days he would refuse and throw a tantrum. After calmly picking up the toys and putting them away, I would state, "No share, no play—then timeout chair." In this way the rule and consequence were stated simply and firmly. I immediately had him sit down in his timeout chair away from his audience—which was his sister. Since he did not want to share, I simply took away the toy. I always told him the reason for the punishment, and once he calmed down, I gave back his toy, but he had to play with his sister for at least a few minutes.

Clarification is important because the child needs to know what they did wrong and why that particular rule is important. Later, when I saw Kenneth sharing with anyone, I would affirm him and comment on how proud I was of him for sharing his toy. Eventually, a child will realize that if they do not listen, a warning from Mom or Dad will be backed by a consistent consequence. They will also realize that doing the right thing is followed by affirmation or hugs because Mom or Dad is pleased with their actions. Thus, the probability of the desired action being repeated will occur.

Level III. If the problem is more chronic, lengthen the timeout or take away playtime for a longer period. If they whine, fuss, or cry, tell them that the timeout will be longer; if necessary, the item will be taken away for hours, days, or permanently. Toddlers understand cause and effect in most situations. Do not give in to a child's drama; their screaming or whining will eventually reach a peak and then it will simmer down. Later, when they are calm, talk about it so your child knows why their behavior was incorrect and what rule was broken. If you give in, you are teaching your child that continuous whining and screaming works, which is detrimental in the long run.

You may want to minimize the length of your child's tantrums as well. If you give in, the tantrums will become longer and longer.

Do not scream or yell at the child during this time because the child will realize their actions are beginning to wear you down. Instead, remain calm and go to the child quietly to reassure them that you are still there. Walking over to your child during their tantrum, repeating the words, "Calm down," and stroking the back of the neck, then walking away lets them know that you care but that you are not giving in. Eventually, you will find that the tantrums will become shorter and shorter until they are extinct.

Always reward your child with hugs, a light rub, or a compliment the moment tantrums cease or when you notice good behavior. This may take a lot of patience on your part because it is difficult to look the other way, but you must establish and reinforce your rules. Remember, you are the boss!

No, No Mommy!—Be Consistent With Your Rules

We will address Level IV later in this segment, but first, I want to expound on behaviors of both child and parent. It is not always the child who needs to change their ways; sometimes, it is Mom and Dad. You may need to use introspect and check yourself to make sure training is being done properly. Inconsistency in implementing and enforcing rules is one of the biggest problems parents face when raising children. A "no" followed by a "yes" to the same rule is confusing to a child. Children are apt to take advantage of poor follow through from parents. It is especially easy to give in to a temperamental child when you are tired, so stay strong, Mom and Dad!

Children also try to divide and conquer by running from one parent to the other to get the desired answer. I know that, even as an adult, I am less apt to follow rules if the enforcer's consequence is unclear. An amount of respect is lost between the enforcer and the enforcee when rules are not consistently managed.

Additionally, problems arise when the enforcer does not practice the rules they are enforcing. We cannot expect our children to follow rules that we would not follow ourselves. If I tell my children to keep their room clean, but my room is covered with dirty clothes and the bed is unmade, then I am not following my own rules.

I see this over and over again as politicians cheat or government vehicles turn on their sirens just to go through a red light for their own convenience. As a child understands his boundaries and parents are consistent with implementation, the child should be rewarded by hugs and kisses or tangible items. They begin to discern and understand what is right and wrong. In addition, outer discipline is not just limited to creating physical boundaries; it can also help the child develop their behavior through copying their parents as role models.

Using Positive Reinforcement to Promote Good Behavior in Early Childhood

The best way to ensure repeated, desired behavior is to use positive reinforcement. When you make a big deal about something your child has accomplished, then they are more apt to do it again because they want to please you. Potty training is an excellent example of how positive reinforcement can be used to promote desired behavior.

Having seven children gave me plenty of opportunities to use trial-and-error strategies to help them graduate from diapers. All of them were potty trained by the time they were two years old. Of course, diapers continued at night when they were asleep in their cribs, but in general they were "diaperless" during the day.

When potty training your child, begin when they are about fifteen to eighteen months old. Buy a child-sized potty chair and begin to use it positivity by making the chair a happy place. Have your child decorate it with stickers. Pin up cute pictures around it. Place it in a high traffic area in your home so your child isn't scared of it. If they see it all the time, then they won't fear it, as it becomes a common thing in the room. Later, it can be moved to the bathroom to show the connection to its real duty. Create a potty song which is sung during and after the potty session. Begin on a weekend when you have more time and patience. Make sure your child drinks a lot of fluids to promote urine. Note that you must prioritize potty sessions and not have so many other things going on in your household that you forget to time your walks to the chair.

Your trips to the potty chair should take place every thirty minutes with two minutes of sit-down time. At the end of each session, use positive reinforcement such as praise and hugs, dancing, or songs, and your child will delight in anticipation as he or she accomplishes the smallest amount or pee-pee or a dot of poop. Start small and build up longer session spans, increasing your child's willingness to sit. The child must connect the cause and effect of the potty session with enjoyment. Go crazy and act silly. Just make the time fun. These sessions will last for weeks and, sometimes, months, but you must be consistent.

Always make a big deal of each session, and let your child know how happy their efforts have made you. When they soil their diaper—and they will—take the dirty diaper with them to the potty chair and help them dump the poop into the potty chair. Again, repeat the silly songs, hugs, and worshipping. Eventually, a poop in the right place will happen. Each time this happens, celebrate. Call Grandma long distance, wrestle on the floor, play a game. Let them know how important this accomplishment has been, and you will find that your child will potty on the chair with more frequent success. Positive reinforcement is the catalyst to more behavior changes.

Developing Outer Discipline through Positive Role Modeling

> *If you don't correct your child, then you don't love your child.*
> *If you do love them, you will correct them.*
>
> ~Proverbs: 13:25

Young children innately depend on their adult to expose them to right and wrong. Learners develop behavior according to what is modeled and accepted by the authority. A conscience or inner discipline is developed slowly over time in reaction to the child's experience around them. Rules should be established consistently so that the child learns what is and is not acceptable. Adults know that a rule without consequence will be broken rather quickly. Community laws require that we, as employed individuals, pay taxes, or we could lose our savings or homes or even go to jail. Without this consequence, we would probably find another way to spend our money. We would then see our neighborhoods in anarchy and realize there are fewer police officers, no fire protection, and less-qualified schooling. Adults understand that rules and laws are necessary in order for our homes and society to function properly. If rules are broken, consequences must be enforced. On the other hand, when compliance or good behavior occurs, there should be reinforcement and affirmation to help continue that behavior.

As the twenty-first century's most important and influential nation, we are losing sight on the importance of rules. The rules are not clear and the consequences are even more unclear. There is now a thin line between acceptable and inappropriate behavior. As I see young children arguing with their parents, whining and throwing tantrums in public, I wonder how these interactions play out at home.

I was at the beach and saw a young child screaming at his father as his lunch was being served. The boy kept screaming, "I don't want this!" The father let him throw a tantrum and the child hit the food out of the father's hand and onto the sand. The father then picked it up and did not scold the child but continued to argue with him. As a teacher I see students demonstrate this same behavior as they begin school.

Americans wonder why we are behind in producing the brightest and the best students in the world. The problem is not in our schools but in how we discipline and reinforce positive behavior at home. Our children seem to be the dictators of what, when, and where things will happen. Somehow, within the recent past, parents have excused themselves from having appropriate power over their children.

The first thing you need to know is that *you* are the parent. You pay the bills, you feed, clothe, and provide many things for your child; therefore, you run the show. Second, your young child is an extension of yourself. You have been given children as a blessing and your role is to teach them lessons that will leave a positive legacy for the next generation. You set the foundation for whether or not your child will be successful. It is your responsibility to show them right from wrong so they can apply it to their lives and be successful. You must remember that you have the power. So, yell it again, "I'm the parent, I have the power!"

Now that you understand this, you must realize that the one in power makes the rules. From the beginning of human and animal kind, the strong have run the show. How and when you distribute that power is the X factor of a well-balanced relationship between parent and child.

Be What You Want Your Kids to Become by Being a Role Model

Your child watches you more than you think. From day to day, children learn as they absorb their surroundings. They subliminally soak up the sights and sounds of their home by innately drawing on the world around them. Many habits are the result of children observing their parents or close family members doing day-to-day activities. Whether we acknowledge it or not, these small behaviors quietly creep into our psyche over the years, especially, when we are young.

One day while my nephew was visiting, I observed him eating at our dinner table. I noticed that his body was hunched over his plate as he gathered all the food on his plate into a big heap. Later, I saw his father eating and realized where my nephew had developed this practice, as I witnessed his dad eating with the same hunched-over style and corralling his meat, peas, and potatoes into a big mountain. Aha! My nephew was a miniature replica of his father. It's true!

Observe your kids one day when they don't notice you watching them and compare them to you. Look at an old video and match your children's mannerisms to your own. More often than not, they sound like you, walk like you, and mimic both your good and bad habits. As a teacher for twenty years, there were many times when I noticed that my students' habits paralleled their parents. Calm parents beget calm children; uptight parents result in uptight and distractible kids. Of course, not everyone has miniature clones walking around, as different temperaments and characteristics set us apart. Many times, the same household will result in different temperaments, but more often than not nurture seems to win out over nature. Understand that you are your child's first teacher. What you do daily is an imprint to their future. So be a positive influence. Your child depends on you to show them the simplest things that we as adults take for granted. You will become the cornerstone of their behavior.

KEEP IT COOL!
LEARN WHAT BEHAVIORS YOU SHOULD PERSONALLY IMPROVE TO BE THE BEST ROLE MODEL FOR YOUR CHILD

Modern society has many conveniences that make our tasks shorter and more efficient. Instead of washing dishes in the morning and doing laundry in the afternoon, we can be driving on the freeway and click a button on our phone to have everything done by the time we reach home. This makes our lives easier, but it also teaches us to want things to be done faster and can create in ourselves a lack of patience as we roll from one task to another. Internally, we are less patient waiting in lines, irritated by having to press phone buttons to speak to automatic robots during customer service calls, and frustrated as we wait for the seconds to tick down on the microwave to finish warming our food. We, unknowingly, have become less patient of others as we try to complete our important to-do lists. These situations can wear us down, and we react in a short-tempered manner because we have learned negative behavior by observing others. Many times, displaced anger builds up over the day. When it is expressed when we get home, confrontations between parents or between parents and their children occur.

Patience is achieved by using awareness of yourself and learning what makes you upset. Learn the triggers that bother you and try to adjust by walking away or breathing through them. You must become bigger than the moment. You need to know that you are in charge of yourself. Use your energy to positively calm yourself rather than using it to get upset and then coming home to vent.

Through personal growth, I have learned to practice cooling down at home and in public so I can teach my children how to confront problems. I taught myself to adjust my reaction toward others in situations in and away from home, and this often resulted in others staying calm around me. Being a "Drama Mama" is a learned behavior, and it is taught by example to children by their parents, especially when out in public.

It is important to model appropriate behavior and to remain calm in public and set expectations so that your children not only know how to act but how to react in all situations. The calmer you appear, the better the chances of raising a calm child. This is taught by being a role model while taking your children with you to places like the store, church, or the mall. These situations will give them more opportunities to observe your appropriate behavior in public. The world is a classroom and every day is a lesson.

I recall one time when I took my three oldest—Solange, five; Kenneth, three; and Melanie, two months—to the hospital for their immunizations. Melanie was in a stroller, while Kenny and Solange tagged along. Kenneth held my hand or the hem of my dress while Solange either walked ahead or alongside, holding the stroller. After finishing with the doctor's appointment, we were waiting on the third floor for the elevator to take us down to the lobby. Being a busy hospital, there were others who were also waiting for one of five elevators to open. When one opened, I pushed the stroller into the elevator and Kenneth walked in as well. Solange started to walk on, but a person already on the elevator decided to get off and nudged her so that person had a clear path off the elevator. Well, as Solange waited for the person to pass, someone on the elevator pushed the button and the doors closed, separating my five-year-old daughter from me. Those on the elevator realized what had happened, and one lady began to scold me while another started to panic. A man attempted to help by trying to push the buttons, which made the situation worse. I was panicked on the inside but knew that I had taught my daughter, "If I ever get separated from you or you get lost, stay put, don't move, and I'll be back!"

Remaining calm on the elevator, I believed that if I got off on the next floor, the elevator could possibly return to my daughter's floor and open without me on it, causing her to panic. Although there were only five floors, it seemed to take an eternity as the elevator stopped at each floor going up and then down, but all I could do was pray, hope, and stay calm. I took a deep breath and contemplated what I should do if she walked away from the point where we had been separated. I figured I needed to have a plan rather than just react. Getting hysterical would not help, and my other children might begin to cry. It did not help that some of the people on the elevator remained to see what would happen.

Finally, the elevator made its way back to the third floor and the door opened. There was my daughter, looking up and searching for my face. Her smile widened as she recognized me as the elevator occupants applauded. I quickly got off and Kenneth began to cry, thinking he was going back to the same doctor to get another shot. Solange just asked with all innocence, "Where did you go? I waited for you. I want to go to get a Happy Meal." (That was our customary procedure after receiving immunizations.)

That day, she remained calm, I remained calm, and everything was okay. I was able to sensibly stay put and anticipate what my daughter might decide to do. I received compliments from my fellow elevator occupants, and I noticed my children looking at me as the people applauded. This was a great moment of learning for my three children, for in that moment they learned what others considered good and positive behavior. Later that day, I explained to my children the positive outcome of the situation and the importance of thinking first before reacting, remembering the rules of staying put, and the use of calmness. I gained respect from others who witnessed this event and, possibly, it helped them in a similar test of their own.

Many years later, I asked Solange what she had been thinking when the doors of the elevator closed on us, and all of a sudden she was without her mommy. She told me that I had always told her to stay put, and she figured I would come back sooner or later. Some years later, using calmness would again benefit my children, as you will eventually read.

Modeling the Rules— "It's the Little Things that Count"

Sometimes, we turn our children into "drama mamas" or "drama kings." Drama mamas or drama kings are those women or men who have little control of their emotions in public places. They are loud and rogue, as they sometimes want negative attention from others as they deal with what should be a private situation. Often, I see children arguing with their parents and bickering with each other over what they are doing or where they are going to go for the rest of their outing. What the parent doesn't realize is that they are setting the future stage for their "drama princesses and princes." Children such as these will become drama queens or drama kings and the cycle will continue. I see parents curse at their children passionately for the simplest things then wonder why their children get in trouble for cursing or being brazen at school.

It is also unfortunate to see parents do dishonest things in front of their children, such as cutting in front of others in line. I have seen parents disrespect their child's teachers without realizing their child is listening and taking mental notes. The child witnesses these encounters and concludes that this behavior is acceptable simply because their parents are doing it. They conclude that this is okay and resolve to disrespect the teacher as well. Then these same parents are puzzled when their child is reprimanded at school for talking back as early as preschool age.

As I observe these instances, I am disappointed because some parents are really dropping a major ball, as they do not realize the negative lessons they are teaching their children. They are either unaware, caught up in the moment's drama, or don't care how their prejudices are affecting their children.

In our household it was always important to follow the rules of respecting others as we would want someone to respect us. Respecting parents should be the foundation for all households. There should be a distinct set of rules within every home. Every home needs rules to assure its proper function and to develop a system of right and wrong. Rules vary from culture to culture, but I believe the basic rule of promoting kindness or love to your fellow man is a foundational fiber woven into almost all beliefs. In every household the parent is the teacher and enforcer of fair rules. The children learn these rules within the home and then later apply them in their own worlds as they grow and experience life.

In my household my mother always had the Bible on the table, and we went to church weekly. The recurring rules of the Ten Commandments, which are based on the respect and love for our fellow man, were always commented on. These rules were clear and covered a wide scope of situations everyone encounters in life. As a parent these rules set boundaries within our household for my children with clear expectations and consequences. These rules were learned at home, reinforced in church, and exemplified by my parents and grandparents as often as possible.

The consistency of implementing these rules through example is hard to do as our children grow. If you want your children to be what you wish them to become, you must be consistent with your own behavior, consistent with the rules, and fair with the consequences. As mentioned before, modeling your rules, such as the avoidance of spreading negative gossip, becomes easier for you if you consider the other person's feelings. Using introspect and empathy before reacting negatively is important for parents to do before teaching children. This is so difficult to do because it is human nature to want to get back at others or make ourselves feel stronger by belittling those around us. Yet, when these moments occur, you can calmly say, "If you can't say something positive about someone, then don't say anything at all." When your children witness you refraining from negative behavior, then they may adopt proactive strategies to react more positively during their own heated situations, which they are bound to encounter.

ROLE MODELING—THE EXPERIMENTAL AGE (THE MID-YEARS, AGES SEVEN TO ELEVEN)

At this point your child has the foundation of their personality and interests laid out. You have been a role model for them, exposed them to daily life, and put them into a school where acquaintances will now become their influence for six hours of the day. Your child will be exposed to friends with different opinions, behaviors, and ways of interaction. School is a microcosm of life.

What your child learns in school will be brought home. This is why you must be consistent with the rules.

Consistency and orderly planning are key elements in raising children. It is important to set boundaries for your children at an early age. When there is a plan at hand, follow it. Make the rules clear within your household. Repeat them constantly; write them down if necessary. Role modeling can aid your children in understanding your expectations, and it is your best bet when helping your children to become the persons you aspire for them to become. If you do not have a good foundation of rules, then they will copy the same up-and-down momentum of behavior that you may exhibit. Show them good morals and ground them with rules that reflect decency toward others.

As mentioned, you can teach your child empathy by repeatedly asking them the simple question, "How would you feel if someone did that to you or spoke to you in that manner?" When asking this, wait for your child's answer. Let them express their ideas so they will comprehend and understand the importance. Expressing intentions and acknowledging results are actions I have used over and over again as a mantra for my seven children. If they can explain it back to you, then they will proactively use good thinking and appropriate behavior when situations occur.

Our families' teachable moments were best discussed on the heels of some situation one of us had just encountered at school, a public place, or when handling a problem at home. Don't push these moments to the side to be discussed at a more convenient time. Talking is important, and skirting issues will fester into more problems later.

To sum it up, behavior is a taught action that develops through young childhood and should mature in methods as your child matures. I learned this technique from my mother. When rules were broken, then consequences were stiff and hard. She would throw guilt my way in a second if I did something like rolling my eyes, talking back, or taking too long to complete a commanded task. These things were considered unacceptable. This would result in a ten-minute lecture and reflection of the fourth commandment—Honor Your Mother and Father—followed by five minutes of "How could you disappoint me like that? Don't you know how hard I work to keep you on the right path?"

As children reach school age and their preteen years, good behavior is best learned when they learn the rules and digest the meaning or place themselves within the rule. They must see the importance and the reason for it. They must state it, learn it, and understand why it is necessary. This is why you must revisit teaching situations at a communal time such as dinnertime or while driving in the car. Point out the wrongdoings that took place and remind your child that actions such as these are even worse when the tables are turned.

I would always go back to the rules and restate them several times. I would recount anecdotes from the past—just like my elder members would do at our dinner table. Reinforcing the need to respect and follow rules improved my children's character. As parents, we also must remind ourselves to reciprocate and respect our children while teaching them and acknowledging their need to be respected. To be considerate of their feelings; to understand and to know them will result in maintaining a mutual and firm relationship.

Family dinners or driving in a car are great times to discuss daily happenings and events which include character building. Invite your children to talk about something that happened and listen to what their lives are really like. Their experiences are far more different and often more difficult than ours were decades ago. I would often use these times to pick my children's brains to learn about peers or pressures and to share my point of view. The room or car would fill with outbursts of laughter as they would say, "I would do this" or "I would not do that." Through these talks, you really get a sense of the future temperament of your child as you listen to them and get a sense of their personalities. Their answers let you know if they are self-centered, generous, or lack confidence, and they give you the opportunity to intervene or just stay back. You cannot change the temperament of your child, but discussions with them can help them become more aware and empathetic toward others.

CONSISTENCY AND THE RULES

> *"Be humble in everything that you do.*
> *The more humble you are the greater you will*
> *become."*

~Sirach 3:17-19

In modeling rules in and out of the home, children develop an understanding of what is expected of them. As previously stated, being a perfect parent at all times is not realistic. However, as mothers we must strive to do the right thing in difficult situations. Looking at you as a role model develops your child's ability toward being respectful. If you are not respectful to others during daily interactions, then your child will be disrespectful as well. Children between the ages of seven and eleven watch to see how the world reacts to them as they try and learn new things. During this time, children test the waters of social interaction with classmates, friends, and others, which builds on their understanding of life. Respect is a learned behavior, so encourage the strategies I have previously mentioned for adults: counting to ten, quickly talking to yourself to make the best decisions, or walking away to get help.

Consistently, talk to your children about bullying. Ask older siblings or cousins to discuss their experiences and describe how they managed their behavior appropriately. As stated before, the examples you set as a parent will likely be the first exposure of proper behavior for your child. I know several parents who tell their children, "If they hit you, then hit them back. Don't be a punk." But as an educator, I can confirm that these teachings often cause the child to get into trouble. Children need to understand that they must deal with situations non-violently and develop wisdom and patience without losing control. Train your child to speak with an adult or teacher before attempting to handle extreme or chronic conflicts on their own.

Each day is a chance to show our children positive behavior. To make decisions of staying in control of emotions gives you time to process the situation so that the loss of composure will not affect others. Life's typical occurrences give us many opportunities to use attributes of honesty, patience, and good judgment. Every situation we are faced with is an opportunity to do the right thing.

For example, have you ever received too much change from a store clerk while shopping? I was in the bank with my children, and the teller gave me $200 extra when counting out a withdrawal. I gave it back to her, explaining the miscalculation and explaining to my children that the extra money would be helpful, but the teller would get in trouble or even be fired. When I gave it back to the teller, she was surprised and graciously complimented me in front of my children. I have no doubt this informal lesson impacted them and increased their capacity to make good character decisions in front of others.

Other ways to demonstrate respectful behavior in front of your children include:

1. Consider other drivers rather than using road rage
2. Curb your use of profanity
3. Encourage sharing
4. Encourage sportsmanship during competitions
5. Acknowledge valor and honesty of others in life

The more positive actions you do in front of your children, the better they will understand that the act of doing right by others is good. Eventually, that good will begin to manifest within your child's thoughts and will become a part of them. They will begin to make their own choices and develop their own personal self-direction. As your child matures, their inner discipline should flourish as parents begin to let go.

INNER DISCIPLINE—THE INNER CHOICE OF BEHAVIOR (AGES EIGHT TO ELEVEN)

> *When parents give their children blessings, they give them strength, but when they curse and nag their children, they destroy their foundation.*
>
> ~Sirach 3: 9

Some children develop inner discipline very young. They find an interest and spend all day doing it. They cannot wait to read that book, build that toy model, or go to the playing field. Many need their parents to direct them by exposing them to different types of activities. This is where years of parental discipline and good role modeling morph into the drive of inner discipline. No one knows exactly when a child will begin to use behavior as his or her own vehicle, but it seems to come around the age of eight or nine. As parents, we can either promote growth or snuff it out. In disciplining your child, set up rules that are fair and reasonable for your children to carry out. Rules should promote behavior which will lead to positive future decisions or choices as your child develops their direction. Overbearing and over-controlling parents who do not exercise tolerance or respect their child's character, needs, and sensitivities foster possible resentment that can cause voids in the parent-child relationship. I recall many tennis matches where I have seen parents scream at their children for losing. The child was embarrassed as the parent nagged them all the way to the car.

Relationships require positive interaction between two people. To belittle your child, especially in front of friends, is a recipe for disrespectful behavior and polarization for years to come. As a parent it is essential that you discipline rather than ridicule your child. Be sensitive to the type, time, and place of punishment, and always reflect upon the rules together to understand and reason through these teachable moments of life.

Finally, make sure you balance discipline with love. Hug your children. Play with them so they see the comical side of you. Be goofy! Being goofy goes a long way. Rules are good, but know when to change it up.

In our house our kids were competing at a high level with other Southern California tennis players for scholarships and college recruitment. We had a few rules whenever our kids competed. One rule was that none of our kids could eat dry cereal before a tennis match. The milk and cereal would cause stomach cramps when they played. Unfortunately, our kids knew that Saturday was the only day that Froot Loops, Lucky Charms, and other colorful, overly sweet cereals were allowed. The rest of the week was oatmeal every morning. So you can imagine that the kids were disappointed when they had to down oatmeal before a tournament. So, some Saturdays after matches, Fred would unexpectedly stop at the store with the kids and surprise them by buying ten boxes of cereal and two gallons of milk, and they would all pig out when they got home. He wanted to enforce the rules, yet show the kids that he cared, and he wanted them to enjoy the rest of their day after the matches. Showing your soft side can make your relationship stronger. Fun is a good and wonderful way to foster future respect.

LEVEL IV: DISCIPLINING—TO SPANK OR NOT TO SPANK (AGES TWO THROUGH TEN)

Now that we have used tolerance and traveled through discipline levels I through III, and we understand that discipline is a balance of love and rules, there are times when a behavior is so severe, such as physically throwing something, destroying something, or hurting one's self or someone else, that the punishment should fit the crime. You must correct the action as soon as possible so that your child understands the severity of what they did. If you are in public when your child acts up then wait until you are both in private. This will also give you a chance to calm down and think about the proper punishment.

Depending on the parent, there are two options of consequence to help correct unacceptable behaviors: spanking or overcorrection. Many see spanking as corporal punishment. Webster's dictionary defines corporal punishment as: *an action applied to the body of an offender, including canning, flogging, or beating.* Let's get this straight. There is no reason why any of these things should be done to any human, let alone a child. Webster defines spanking as: *hitting the buttocks with an open hand.* GoodParent.org states that spanking and corporal punishment are not equal terms. Spanking is not slapping, hitting with an object, or beating. To me, spanking should be used as a punishment for the most severe of actions. It is a way to impress upon a child the importance of a rule so they will remember it for their own safety. Firmly hitting a child on their buttocks several times in the privacy of your own home reflects the severity of the rule broken and will not hurt the child. The child needs to fear the punishment or they will repeat the infraction.

When I was seven, my sister and I wanted to visit our neighborhood friend who lived across the street near the corner. Rather than walk to the corner as usual, I made the decision to get to my friend's house faster than my sister. I ran across the street without looking for oncoming traffic. A driver had to slam on his brakes to avoid hitting me. When we returned home, my sister, of course, told my mother, who then spanked me. My mom knew I had tried this before, so she told me, "I'd rather you have a little pain now and remember what you did rather then get hurt badly or even killed later."

If the child's behavior affects their safety or the safety of others, you need to match the behavior with an action that will be remembered. My older children were spanked only twice in their lives before the age of nine. The behaviors were serious enough that I really felt it was necessary. On one instance, Solange and Kenny were playing tag with typical sibling competitiveness. Kenny was teasing her, as brothers do. He dared her to throw a shoe at him. She did, and as he ducked, the shoe hit and shattered our plate glass window in the living room. A large sheet of glass barely missed Kenny as it fell to the floor.

Though it was an unintentional accident, I had stressed to both of them on previous occasions to never throw any objects at each other, especially in the house. I sent them to their rooms so I could calm down and clean up. I spanked both of them. I never injured them, but it made them cry and made an impression on them they still remember today. I made sure they understood the danger of the moment and the reasoning behind my established rules.

Every time I disciplined on any level, I asked each child, "What did you do? How did you break my rule?" In this case, they were both able to explain to me that the falling glass would have hurt them.

Never discipline a child when you are emotionally out of control, frustrated with other things in your life, or tired. Think of what consequence fits the behavior, and enforce it. I never screamed or nagged but consistently taught them what was expected, how to behave, and to think before making choices. Seldom yet necessary spanking created boundaries in my children's minds, which made them think twice. As they grew older, they relayed these rules to their younger siblings, who then knew not to cross certain lines; thus, very seldom did we get to Level IV.

If you prefer not to spank your children, overcorrection is another appropriate punishment for Level IV or less severe behaviors. Whenever the negative behavior occurs, make the child recompense by having them do the opposite action a number of times. Many teachers do this so their student will think twice before breaking rules. For example, if a child throws something, such as a book, have them place ten, twelve, or more books on the floor and make the child pick them up. And you say, "Since you like throwing books so much, now you can pick up even more."

When my daughter Solange was five, she didn't want to drink milk with her meals. She wanted soda instead. Our rule was to drink milk with every meal; sodas were limited throughout the week. When I told her she could not drink soda at dinnertime, she threw her milk on the floor. I made her get out of the chair and clean it up with a towel until the floor was spotless. As she cried, I asked her, "What did you do wrong?" She told me with a clear understanding what she had done wrong. To her the punishment seemed unfair, but she later realized that if she repeated her action, she would have to clean it all up again. The mundane aftermath of overcorrecting by immediately making her clean up the floor, the chair, and the splattered cabinets made an impact on her. She never threw down her milk again.

At school, when one of my students aggressively hits another student, I make the child write an apology note every day for a week during the time they would generally play. Children hate mundane things that take away from their fun, and they will remember the next time simply because they do not want to repeat the punishment.

If you choose to do either one of these punishments, positive interaction will be necessary. Let the child understand that pleasing you is more important, and the joy of you being pleased outweighs the fear of being spanked or overcorrected. As the child matures, the inner discipline, which has been learned from years of disciplining, will help them with decisions on whether to engage in negative or positive behavior. Above all, make sure you positively reinforce when your child decreases extreme negative behavior; they will recognize you are pleased and will be less likely to repeat the errant behavior. As stated before, verbal understanding is important, especially after Level IV, so that your child can internalize the problem, know the rule and the reason, and not repeat the behavior.

ADOLESCENCE AND TEEN YEARS
(AGES TWELVE THROUGH EIGHTEEN)

Teens want to test the boundaries of supervision. No matter how much you think your teen may be going in the wrong direction, the crazy haircuts, piercings, and other new interests are all telltale signs of their budding independence. The once lovely child you bounced on your knee can battle with you over the smallest things during this time of transition. During adolescence, their need to break away from being a child and become a young adult tends to trump everything else, even their relationship with you. Disciplining your teenager with well-developed rules and consistent implementation is just as important as it was when they were younger. Keep in mind that the balance between supportive love and correction is different for each child and will change as they grow older.

Each of our children required a different balance of discipline. Preteen boys and girls have different problems. Varying temperaments demand different levels of sensitivity and flexibility. The expectations within our household created a general foundation, yet some personalities did not always result in compliance. With our girls, Melanie was very easygoing and gave us few problems, while Michelle was more headstrong and needed more explanation of the rules. We needed to give her room to debate and express her thoughts so that she understood the reasons behind the rules. Rules need to make sense to teenagers, so go over them long before it is time to enforce them.

You must understand that the same rules and expectations of childhood do not apply to the teen years. Yes, they should be required to help out more around the house, but most rules will probably be geared toward activities away from the home.

You must learn to trust them as they learn to drive and begin working part time. You must also learn to trust them and have faith that you have given them the best foundation for making good decisions. Ask questions daily, and try to have communal times as much as possible. If rules are broken, then grounding is your best bet. Never become physical. Do not spank or hit your teenager. Although their sense of rationale is still young, they are too old for that. Communication should continue no matter how distant a child may seem. Keep them involved in positive groups and consider family counseling as a way to work through extreme problems.

Chapter 3

Adolescence and Teen Years
(Ages Twelve through Eighteen)

THE REALITY AND NEED FOR RELATIONSHIP AND DISCIPLINE

Puberty can be a tricky time of growth as your child begins to become a young man or woman. They change both physically and emotionally as they mature. Their challenges range from menstrual cramps to pimples, to developing muscles and sprouting hair in all sorts of new places. Puberty can also be very emotional as your child searches for independence and the need to fit in with others their age. It is time to experiment with the open door of life as your child takes everything you have taught them and applies it in their own ways.

Parents tend to be wary of this time. They keep their distance or brush over situations, believing that aloof behavior is typical at this age. Within our home we were fortunate to go through mild emotional puberty stages. Up until the age of seventeen, all seven of our children were all under our roof, so they had to abide by our rules. Melanie wanted to wear makeup, but we didn't let her. To satisfy this urge, I bought her nude lip gloss and let her know that her eyes were naturally beautiful. We also allowed her to get an entire collection of flavored lip glosses so she could alternate daily. This kind of give and take is important because flexibility and the tug of independence must be recognized. She wanted makeup; I gave her an option while still denying the initial issue. Fred also flattered her by letting her know that her eyes were already beautiful and that she did not need to use makeup to look pretty.

At times there was moodiness, but mostly, my girls focused on clothes and combining outfits during those years. The boys seemed to be focused on building their body muscles through lifting weights outside. I guess the bottom line was that they wanted to look nice to the opposite sex. I believe the foundation of rules implemented in our home for many years kept possible volatile adolescent and teenage episodes at a minimum. During this time it is important for parents to be role models by setting examples and limitations. Our children knew there was consistency implemented, so we could focus on other areas of emotional needs in order to promote their independence.

During the period of early-teen growth, I believe the biggest challenge is personal self-esteem. One of the emotional trampolines of puberty is the overwhelming desire for the acceptance of others. Many preteens, including myself, struggled to gain peer acceptance. Confusion of one's awkward changes in appearance, finding friendships, and developing relationships affect our feelings of self-worth. In turn, the way you feel about yourself affects how others treat you. If you are constantly affected by others' perceptions of you, you will always be chained by their opinions and comments. Once people realize you are vulnerable and can be manipulated, some will leverage their power over you. They will feed upon your lack of confidence, as they feel stronger when they are around you, especially in the preteen and teen years. As parents, we need to help our children project positive feelings about themselves so they feel more confident in the things they do. Parents are the cheerleaders and comforters young people need, but this can be hard, especially when the child is emotionally distant or combatant.

ADOLESCENTS AND TEENS NEED YOUR DAILY SUPPORT

Try to think way back to when you were a teen, with all the social pressures and emotional moments. In middle school and high school, there are many issues which can be stressful. Home should be a haven of refuge for your child; it should provide a sense of safety. So Mom, please do not come home from work or an outing like a sergeant in the army, fussing about why someone has not completed something or that chores are not yet done.

As moms, we are often reactionary because we expect to be respected. When we have a bad day, we take it out on those who are less of a threat to us or less apt to rebuke our opinion. Though it is important that certain expected household responsibilities get done, you should first acknowledge your children when you arrive home after work and let them know you are glad to see them. Screaming at your teen or walking through your home getting everyone riled up leads to dramatic power struggles. Speak calmly and refer to schedules that should have been made clear at an earlier time. Rules should be discussed while cell phones and computers are turned off to allow all parties to devote their undivided attention to the conversation. Pause, take ten minutes, have a snack together, and discuss the day's events. This gift of love that only a parent can provide only takes a few moments out of a busy day. Hug your children. If they are too big to hug then tell them that you need a hug, that you had a lousy day, and that you need a little love. This should start when your children are younger. If you have an older one, sit down and tell them briefly about your day or your new routine, and ask them one thing that went right in their day. When your relationships are strengthened through common discussion, you will see that the children are more apt to complete their chores out of a genuine desire to please you.

Having a weekly chore chart posted helped immensely in our home. I taped it in a high traffic area so the children could not miss it when they walked by. This cut down on arguing, as everyone knew what was expected of them. Sometimes, things did not always run smoothly. Late library nights, tennis matches, and impromptu visitors caused talk or chore time to be pushed back. Chore trading was common, depending on homework demands. Remember, schedules should be used as a tool to organize life, not dictate it. Flexibility may be needed from time to time, and that's okay.

Teach Adolescents to Ask for Help

Adolescents need to learn how to ask for help. During this time of life, a child must decipher what they have learned at home and apply it to their current, more independent life.

Young people harbor stress. The issues of bullying, the need for acceptance, and the pain of rejection—all this can be so intense that adolescents and younger teens may feel overwhelmed. They may turn inward and turn everyone else away by confining themselves to their room. In addition to this, the access to phones and computers may lead your child to engage in social media, which can be a blessing or an addition to their stress. Children are often confused and may question their own existence.

It is a parent's job to help and support them during this time while still being in control of the rules. It is a very tricky balancing act. My best advice is to begin encouraging them from a young age. Develop a relationship so they know you are there as a resource during the strains of life. Begin to use your sensitivity radar to notice extreme changes in behavior, such as despondency or mood swings. Sometimes, young teens are better served when you send the cavalry of siblings or trusted mentors in so that your child has an avenue to spout his or her needs without feeling uncomfortable. A sensitive conversation can lead to a balance of emotions that may help relieve an unstable teen's moment. If you do not create a pathway for honest communication, then your child will find someone else who will listen to them, someone who might provide the wrong type of support.

BUILDING SIBLING BONDS EARLY LEADS TO ADOLESCENT SUPPORT LATER

When my children were young, my husband and I always encouraged them to play in the same room with each other. They had to work out their problems, and only an intense squabble would lead to Fred or me intervening. As they became more involved in tennis, their daily schedules became so tight that there was not enough time to argue. If they needed advice about simple issues at school or tennis, their father or I would tell them to ask their brothers or sisters. Later, I would always drift among the kids to see what was going on in case I needed to become more involved. We wanted them to interact and depend upon one another. As they grew up together, they were continuously involved in each other's lives. These relationships were reinforced during communal times in the car rides home.

When Melanie began to win her tennis matches, Kenny felt the victory as well. As she increased her wins, his confidence grew, and she grew in other areas as she developed tennis smarts and "strategy consciousness." She then passed on her support to Christopher, the next in line. The same support system was evident in completing homework, projects, or on difficult days when some comic relief was needed. Silly bantering, imitating each other, or karaoke moments would lighten the load. When your children are young, simple times, such as playing outside, movie nights, games nights, or short road trips can be the catalyst for stronger bonds that will last a lifetime.

Develop a rapport of trust and respect through years of talking as they grow. Teens love to talk and they crave independence, but they also want the love and acceptance of their parent. Keep them involved in activities, even if it requires you to drive them everywhere, so they may develop a sense of accomplishment and self-worth. Being happy at any age comes from within—from inner discipline. Relationships are formed as one falls down but is upheld by others. Use wisdom in understanding their point of view and understand that this part of motherhood is a balancing act of accepting their changes, dispensing appropriate discipline, and being the support your child needs when times are tough.

ADOLESCENTS, RESPECT PARENTS; PARENTS, RESPECT THE ADOLESCENT

It is important that you continue to implement the rules within your home and not change them just because your teen has difficulty accepting them. Remember those temper tantrums when your toddler was first exploring the world? Well, puberty produces the same trial and error toward growing independence. As parents you tend to have less energy as your children get older. But as they become more mobile, you must stay aware of what they are doing. Know their school schedules and visit their teachers; even if you must take off from work.

I also required myself to know or at least meet my children's friends. Occasionally, I heard the beeping of a car horn outside our home as someone came to pick up one of my kids. It was my job to know who was picking them up and where they were going. So I would walk outside and meet the driver. Sometimes, it was embarrassing to my child, but eventually, the driver would get used to seeing me poking out my head and would just say hello. Seeing a parent involved is a friendly reminder to your children that while Mom might be under the radar, she is still watching with care.

Here are a few rules that we enforced in our home:

1. No house parties. My children were not allowed to go to house parties because there are too many things that can go wrong in a house full of teenagers. With cell phone access, party invites often transferred from friends to strangers within minutes. Even if I knew the host or their parents, I disallowed attending the party. Regardless of tears, the answer was always no.

2. None of our seven kids were allowed to drive before the age of seventeen. Los Angeles has too many cars and distractions. I would give them a ride or let an older brother or sister drive them to wherever they needed to go. There were many nights when their father and I would drive them to dances or activities then wait outside or be there to pick them up.

3. My girls were required to dress with integrity. If you dress respectfully, then you will be treated with respect. No halter tops, booty skirts, or boobs hanging out to enhance flirtation. I let my girls know they did not need to look loose and available. Such behavior might be popular, but self-respect is priceless.

4. Boyfriends and girlfriends were not allowed before the age of sixteen. This was the toughest on Solange because she was the oldest and the first to go out with boys. She liked this one boy down the street. He would come over, and they went to a few dances. I wanted her to be aware of the

coming-of-age problems that kids face these days. We had discussions about relationships, but she wasn't allowed to go on dates until she was sixteen. He was seventeen and already had a car. Once dating was allowed, our 11:30 p.m. curfew became the cause of many confrontations.

Through these bouts of independence, I learned that calm talk was more effective than pulling rank and issuing power. Since Fred steered clear of this area, I found I needed to take time and develop our mother/daughter relationship on these sensitive levels that were uncomfortable but necessary. Without bugging her too much, I would ask her the next day about how her date went, and we would discuss what she liked about him. I talked about my own relationship with her father when we were dating at her age. She and I would talk about sex and how it was a special commitment. I advised her to come to me if she decided to become sexually active so we could seek medical assistance together. We discussed her knowledge of friends' sexual activities and how an unwanted pregnancy could derail her future plans of college and the potential for a comfortable financial future. We discussed some of my former students and their struggles once they became pregnant and had babies while in their teens. I made sure these personal conversations were timed right, and I never forced answers. Sometimes, I would be the only one talking, but over time she began to listen and understand that I was coming from a place of concern and wisdom.

To my relief, she broke up with her boyfriend after a few months. I knew my daughter was getting older and would meet other young men. When she turned seventeen and went away to college, I made sure she began taking birth control and that she understood the importance of her partner using condoms and the possibility of sexually transmitted diseases. This was not permission for her to have sex, but rather that I understood that sex was a possibility and I wanted her to be safe and careful.

While I'm sure there are many stories I have never heard and may not ever want to hear, I know that our talks will become anecdotes she will use to teach her own children in the future.

5. Cell phones were not allowed before graduation from high school. It was an unnecessary distraction that pulled my kids away from what they should be doing. Parents should show their children proper cell phone time management by making sure that certain times—such as at school or when driving—are times of focus. Also, prepaid cell phones could only be used in case of an emergency. It is still a rule that when we get together at a restaurant or family dinner, Mom always stresses, "No cell phones, please!" Other conversations and the internet can wait until later.

"The Talk"

I believe that sex is an important and consistent topic which should be discussed once your children turn eleven years old. I made sure to discuss the topic of abstinence with all my children. The kids called it "The Talk." It was weird at first for me because my own mother didn't say much other than, "Just don't do it!" I did not want my children to become a part of the growing trend of teen pregnancies. I wanted them to go through their younger years without the stress associated with teen pregnancy. I prepared myself with statistics on disease to help them understand the realities of going to bed with someone and the diseases that could occur with unprotected sexual activity.

I must admit that a good incentive toward postponing sexual activity in our home was purposefully making my children help with caring for new babies who came along. Looking after their younger siblings helped my children see the confining nature and responsibility of having babies. Solange, Kenneth, Melanie, and Chris grew up as impromptu diaper changers and baby feeders when I needed help. During "The Talk," I had them recall the many times they had to calm their screaming baby sister or brother. Lastly, I found that once I set the tone of adolescent behavior within our home, my younger children knew what was to be expected as they watched their older sister or brother go through that same stage in life. That is why it is so important to establish an early relationship between siblings so they can be mentors to each other and be willing to learn from one another.

DISCERNING THE MEDIA TO SUPPORT YOUR TEEN

Many teens I've tutored listen to music with lyrics that address girls as "bitches" or talk about how the latest star lost his virginity at eight years old. I ask them how they feel about sex and I find that many feel overwhelmed and pressured to do things far before they should, just for popularity's sake. I always discuss the importance of respecting their own bodies and to never be the object of someone else's pressure or selfish pleasure.

It is the parents' role to strengthen their children's self-respect. From an early age, parents need to use proper role modeling regarding what their child looks at and listens to. Using discretion when selecting what channels to watch or what music to listen to helps the child realize how certain types of media degrade the importance of the human body and promote sexual activity. Don't get me wrong, what Mom and Dad see in the privacy of their own bedroom is up to them, but you must let your children know that younger teens should not be looking at inappropriate sexual content. Young minds are immature and confusion can lead to experimental behavior, which is dangerous, both physically and emotionally. By discussing discretion, your child is more apt to make wiser decisions as they are exposed to different things every day. It makes them think about the choices of how to handle themselves.

Television, radio, and the internet send so many mixed signals and guide our children on how to dress and act. I always had two TVs and one computer in a general part of the house so I could walk through at any time and glance at what my children were looking at, especially during primetime hours. I wanted my children to be as normal as their friends, so I let them watch videos and various movies on the one set in our den, but I monitored it as much as I could by walking in and out. I would turn off any of the videos that had too much adult content in them. I would pause it and ask, "Do you think this is appropriate?" My intention was to get them to use their own discretion instead of enforcing my own. I let them watch movies of their choice so long as they were no higher than a PG-13 rating—and sometimes, I turned those off as well. Music video stations were allowed on Saturdays or Sundays, maybe both. I didn't want them to resent me as a parent, but I was strict on the amount of viewing time. To see their favorite musical artists, the latest clothes, or music kept them in the loop, but I also kept a loop around the situation in order to avoid possible twisted indulgence. Teaching your children to discern is an ongoing lesson that will, hopefully, eventually seep into their adulthood.

In addition to monitoring their viewing time, I also exposed them to programs that were important. I learned a lot about the world, politics, art, and important issues because, as a child, my siblings and I were required to sit and watch certain televised events, like the movie "Roots." I remember feeling imprisoned as I was told to sit and watch, but after the first episode, I found it was important to open my mind to my own cultural heritage and the American tragedy of slavery. I still use the movie "Roots" in my classroom to educate my students. As a child I was also commanded to watch the political conventions of both parties during election years, and it gave me an understanding of various perspectives. So when Barack Obama was elected, my children had already been following the election. They knew the problems facing their futures in the job market and the impact of the economy on their father's troubled business.

When watching TV with your kids, act dumb and have them teach you something as a way to spark conversation. Children love to be the wiser ones. In my case I did not have to play dumb because I really needed help with technology. I depended on them to help me with the television remote and the computer for my schoolwork, among other things. My kids had to practice patience with me, but it was good for them to see what I had to go through. Let them know how much you appreciate their help and that *you* need *their* advice and help at times. It helps promote empathy and a sense of equality in the home.

Lastly, I am very fortunate to be married. Although it can be a challenge at times, we have tried to show our children that a family lifestyle of both parents living with their children is a blessing. Only fifty percent of adults get married, and half of those marriages end in divorce. We tried to show our children, especially our teenagers, that we could communicate and work out our issues, especially during our hectic schedules and times of financial troubles. We never fought in front of them. However, there were times when they knew we were avoiding each other.

Displaying romance in front of your children is a difficult wire to walk if you are divorced and/or dating. Just remember that your children are watching you.

A Recap on Teen Conduct and Discipline

1. Set the rules for your teenager with reasoning and proper flexibility.

2. Try to limit promiscuous language or profanity within the home.

3. If you are dating, keeping your relationship private and out of the home is important. Find outside places for physical romance. Remember, your children are observant and you are setting an example for their future relationships. Keep your kids in the discussion loop in case your relationship becomes more serious.

4. Don't be naïve about the amount of information children absorb from movies, music, television, and the internet. Your children are bombarded with misguided information and enticing content. Sexual curiosity can turn into uneducated actions that could change the direction of their lives. Combat ignorance with education.

5. Have an established routine of communicating with your children about relationships. Doing so will make the discussion of physical relationships easier to navigate in the future.

6. Get to know your children's friends and teachers. If you can, meet your friends' parents as well. Get phone numbers and communicate so you can keep track of your children's activities when they are with their friends.

7. Grant your children access to information regarding birth control as they reach preteen years or adolescence.

8. Keep your children busy so they spend their time working and being productive. Help them with their goals rather than allowing idle time for surfing the internet or hanging around with negative influencers.

Learn Forgiveness toward Your Adolescents and Teens

Above all, use forgiveness in disciplining your children, especially during their preteen and teen years. No matter what happens in life, understand that your child will always be your flesh and blood. You must understand that everyone makes mistakes, and life is about running the race. In my personal relationship with God, I know I am His child, although I have not been perfect. We all have done things beneath our own expectations of ourselves. The problems of life and negative influences guide us away from our best direction and choices. Our children are gifts from God. They may take us to the edge of patience, but we must practice developing patience as God is patient with each of us. Our children may hurt us more than anyone else possibly could. They may be involved in things that may drag our relationship down for years. Yet they are our children and we must learn to forgive them because family is necessary for our emotional survival. If you have been separated from your child for years, learn to pray that you will be open to them, and be a role model of forgiveness. If it still doesn't occur, then continue to pray for your child. Learn to look above the problem that entangles them and ask for divine guidance so your child will be directed toward a better path.

I know a mom whose child has been a homeless addict for fifteen years. She tells me that her home is always open to her child to get help. She prays for her child daily. She knows that prayer keeps a motherly relationship going, at least in one direction. I recently heard that her child, who is now forty, is checking herself into a drug and alcohol rehabilitation center. For her, the future will always be uncertain, as addictions can ravage the physical and mental, but hope and support can change the bleakest situation.

The physical bond between a mother and child will always exist as long as there is life. The emotional bond is built upon the physical connection of birth. Your child will always need you. Always try to communicate and get along because you will eventually need each other. My mom is now in her eighties and depends on me for physical, financial, and emotional support. She needs me now to drive her everywhere, keep her finances straight, and be her emotional lifeline. Whatever life has thrown our way, I have learned to forgive and to practice patience with her. She did the same for me when I was a challenging child; now we must both move on and go forward. I pray that my own children see me patiently dealing with my mom as she lives with us and understand that when the time comes, they will need to help me as well.

My mom and me.

PART II

TEACHING THE FOUR CORNERSTONES OF SUCCESS

Chapter 4

Teaching the Four Cornerstones to Success

Beyond role modeling right and wrong, our job as mothers is to teach our children how to develop successful habits. These habits develop over years of implementation and become part of our constitution. More than anything, parents must focus upon and teach their children ways to become successful. We want them to become independent and take care of themselves and their families. These four areas of teaching are critical for a productive future:

1. Teaching acceptable Social Skills
2. Teaching your children about Positive Finance
3. Teaching them the Importance of Prayer
4. Teaching your children about Setting Goals

TEACHING TEENS POLITENESS AND COURTESY

Teaching teens good social skills is imperative for their success. Therefore, you must emphasize the acts of being polite and courteous. This will help your teen immensely with their independence and self-esteem, as they will one day go out into a fiercely competitive world. The current younger generation differs from preceding generations because they must also compete in an international job market. Later, I will discuss the importance of your children being prepared for that job market, but first, I want to emphasize the importance of being personable.

Companies and colleges see hundreds of applications listing the same amount of education and experience. But the "X" factor that puts a person above the rest often includes recommendations and references from past employers, teachers, supervisors, and/or friends. You must help your child build character. Being polite and using good manners leaves a lasting impression on others. The world has become faster and more demanding. We tend to become more self-centered as we have less time to complete all the things on our agendas. But humans are social beings. When we are trying to get something done, being personable can work magic with others. Proper socialization skills create a world with more positive interactions. It leads to better networking and promotes problem-solving abilities. When you model positive social skills to your children, they learn how to deal with others and understand the importance of communication for their own benefit. Some basic elements of good social skills that you should teach your children are:

1. Wait your turn to talk during a conversation
2. Intently listen to others
3. Think before responding during a conversation
4. Smile and say hello to those with whom you are familiar
5. Offer assistance to those who may need your help

Waiting your turn can be irritating. We need to practice being patient and respectful with others. If you react negatively in front of your children by complaining unnecessarily, you may create impatient children. Just as an athlete trains his or her body to increase endurance for distance or speed, a person can increase their tolerance and patience level when reacting to events going on around them. One person may only be able to tolerate standing in a bank line for ten minutes before beginning to fidget and complain, while another person may wait and understand that bank lines are inevitable. Thus, we can teach our children tolerance toward people and daily situations. Assimilating to different situations will increase the chances of the moment ending positively without your blood pressure going up.

In order to be respected by others, conversational etiquette is essential to politeness and courtesy. I have emphasized to my children numerous times that they must practice good conversational skills in order to progress in this world. People will respect you more and treat you better if you present yourself intelligently and are courteous during conversations. Make sure you:

1. Look at the face of the person to whom you are speaking. Make the other person feel respected by listening to them, no matter how much you disagree with them. Wait for them to finish what they are saying and follow the progression of the conversation. Avoid letting your mind drift away. Avoid answering cell phones or texting during conversations. Aside from being disrespectful, the person you are engaging with might feel less important or unworthy of your time.

2. Always think before speaking because you do not want to take the risk of sounding unintelligent or saying something that will come back to hurt you. If you are not sure what to say, then just nod your head in agreement, politely state that you are not sure, or simply state, "I will have to get back to you later."

Always smile and say hello daily to those you see, especially at work. Small talk promotes a friendly social atmosphere. People will remember you and be more apt to help you when you need a favor, advice, or need to network toward advancement in life.

3. Tell your children to think before they respond during a conversation; especially if they are upset and want to retort. Teach them techniques of calming down in order to get what they want. In some extreme cases, it may save their life. How many times have we heard on the news about a shooting occurring after a heated argument due to someone pulling out a gun and reacting before thinking?

4. Finally, good social skills include *helping others* without expecting something in return. By unexpectedly offering help to someone, the person feels surprised and will think greater of you for taking your time and assisting them.

REAPING THE BENEFITS OF GOOD SOCIAL SKILLS

Sooner or later, your children will connect with people who appreciate their steadiness; thus, they will want to help them in various ways. This is why it is so important to take young children with you when you go on errands. They see how to act properly through your example as you demonstrate and discuss situations with them.

As the years passed, my children met many people through their tennis experiences, school, and helping others through community service. As other people remembered my children, they were able to help them get jobs, recommendations, scholarships, and internships. The positive, lasting impression my children left over the years has led to an overflowing amount of opportunities. Over time, my husband and I have received compliments about our children and their polite, well-mannered personalities.

We had two children attend Howard University and one attend Georgetown University—she later transferred to Howard—all of them on full, four-year academic or tennis scholarships. This was partially due to my first son, Kenneth, making calls on his brother's behalf. Kenneth began the Howard University/Brown Family Legacy that later influenced his brother's and sister's attendance. Kenneth played in the #1 position on the tennis team and became the team captain, guiding other young players as a role model. Although he had academic challenges due to learning difficulties, in addition to a packed academic schedule, he worked hard and made it through. This opened the door for Coach Larry Strickland to review Kenneth's brother Chris, whose athletic and academic abilities led the coach to offer Chris a full, four-year scholarship. Additionally, the coach's positive experience with my sons led to the recruitment of my daughter Michelle to Howard University from Georgetown to play tennis. He offered her a full scholarship, too.

The ability to make a good impression and to gain trustworthiness from others takes time, but these attributes will serve you well as you advance when you run your race. Melanie, who was very friendly, created a tennis team at her high school. She was interested in nursing, so the coach at her high school contacted the coach from Prairie View A & M, who later came out to recruit her. He immediately offered her a full, four-year scholarship. Richard Williams, of the Venus and Serena Williams Tennis Academy in our neighborhood park, invited the Virginia State University coach to see our twins play, and they received partial, four-year scholarships. All and all, my family's involvement in tennis over a span of twenty years saved us over a million dollars in college tuition and fees. Although they were prepared athletically and academically, it was our children's personalities that helped others remember them and consider them when opportunities arose.

WATER THE FLOWERS

The world is a smaller place than you think. Although it may be difficult to be polite at times, you must follow the old cliché, "You reap what you sow." Remember, the person with whom you were friendly or unfriendly with today may be the one person you need help from in your future. As a teacher, I have seen teacher's assistants become teachers, then principals, and then superintendents. Do not let a bad relationship come back to bite you on the butt. I always tell my children to "water the flowers." You will always reencounter people who knew you through school, job, or activities. There is always a chance that the circles of our lives will overlap. A quick hello email, a card, or a phone call every few months reminds others about you in a positive way. Taking the time to remember those around you helps to foster relationships that can be beneficial in the long run.

On the other hand, I have always told my children that people will also remember you if you spread negative conversation or gossip. Negative emotional scars are remembered long after the incident. I asked my children if they remember any bullies growing up. Decades later, they could still recall details of incidences involving others being cruel to them. Fear and trauma keep psychiatrists very busy, as people pay great amounts of money to have someone assist them through the healing process. The scars of irrelevant gossip can eventually work their way back to their source.

As a mentor, always refrain from gossiping in front of your children or friends. Children will learn to gossip if they believe it is the norm. I never let my children buy grocery store tabloid newspapers or look at television shows that bash or degrade other people. Everyone's lives are impacted by unfortunate events. No matter how rich or poor, everyone will encounter their share of dilemmas.

Avoid highlighting others' misfortune or pain to make you feel superior. Remember, your time will come, and you will appreciate people helping you rather than gossiping about it to others.

When my husband's business ended during the recession, we had to endure the embarrassment of gossip. As we faced financial problems because of the business failure, we appreciated when people helped us even more. My sister-in-law Sheree bought my younger children bikes for Christmas. I shared with my children the importance of how most people did not put us down during this tough time. I told them that we had helped others, and in return they were helping us. As you "water the flowers," others will return favors and show the bloom of that flower. While driving back and forth in the car so many times to so many practices, tournaments, and countless weekend events, we did not have a movie or video game going in the car; instead, we spent the time talking to each other. I always referred to those small events or reverse favors as grace coming back around in various forms.

Finally, part of teaching your children appropriate manners starts at home with you being kind to other family members. My husband and I made sure to never belittle others, especially, family, which could cause dissention. Emphasize the importance of the foundation of family life. You should have others, especially, your family, to fall back on.

SERVICE TO OTHERS—GIVING BACK

One of the most important things you can do to foster tolerance and patience within your child is to expose them to community service. The example of serving others brings out the good in all of us. By serving or helping others with your ability, time, or monetary excess, you step out of the need to satisfy yourself, and you help make this world a better place. Your children will benefit and become more sensitive toward others as they see you give of yourself to others.

You must first find something that you enjoy. I always enjoyed music, so I coupled that with my natural knack for mentoring children and got involved in the church choir. Helping with the church choir required me to renew my childhood piano skills so I could assist the choir when needed. Once they hired a permanent pianist, I continued to assist the director by helping her discipline and guide the children during practices. I accompanied my children every Friday to practice, as did other parents. Of course, there were many Fridays when we could not make it, but we tried our best to make as many events as possible.

Choir is not the only way you can get your child involved with the community. By donating clothes, or even sacrificing a Saturday for community causes, a child may experience the intrinsic joy one inherits through giving to others. In addition to the choir, my children volunteered to set up tennis tournaments, worked at church, and tutored children in the community.

I always emphasize that volunteering is the best way to give back to the community. Have your children start young and help them find something they are interested in. From cleaning up trash on the beach, to food banks, there is always something to do somewhere. Once a child is involved in service to others, it awakens their mind to become sensitive to others and the realization that life can be harsh. It helps them to look at life through another perspective, and they realize that even children have the power to help others. For the past ten years, my son Kenneth has worked with his church to help orphans of Benin, Africa, who have been ravaged by the effects of HIV. He collects funds and clothing donations and sends them to the church there.

Chapter 5

Teaching Your Children and Teens about Money

Many have asked how my husband and I financially survived supporting such a large family. Truth is, we lived very modestly, yet comfortably. We were happy with the same TV and car for years. We worked hard to begin our business, and we managed our expenses so I could stay home and raise our children until the twins were four years old. Everything didn't have to be new, and we did not saturate our children with every activity, but we spent money on special events that occurred annually. My kids can still remember when we all went to Disneyland and stayed two days at the Disneyland Hotel. They were floored by the excitement. We coordinated with our relatives, who also spent two days running around with us. There is nothing like being at an amusement park and hotel with twenty cousins. We also coordinated overnight snow trips and camping trips. These family trips were priceless and the fun of being with the family provided much bang for the buck. The experiences helped to shape our family's camaraderie as a support network and kept my children involved with each other as they had fun together.

Our toughest financial time came during the recession years. During 2007-2008, the stock market crashed, causing many to lose jobs and small businesses to close. Like many other Americans, our family experienced hardship. We had already been experiencing financial difficulties since 2003, as many small businesses like ours had to downsize or close. The trickle-down effect of businesses closing due to bankruptcy contributed to our woes, as many of our accounts receivable could not pay us. Consequently, we had to move into my childhood home to help balance our money and to help my mom, who was about to retire. We transferred our children from private parochial schools to charter schools, and I continued my college classes to earn my credentials in order to qualify for a better position.

I believe the way you handle a situation depends on your frame of mind and your attitude. Our family's lifestyle was humble already, but moving into my mom's home with seven children was no joke. We had been helping Mom financially for years, and it did not make sense to continue paying her mortgage while simultaneously renting a single-family home. In order to pay off our business loans, we had to consolidate expenses, sell our machinery, our business, and, eventually, the building we had worked so hard to buy.

Our children knew we were struggling, but since we had lived modestly for years, our established habits and faith helped us to financially reboot ourselves. Fred, using his design, technical, and mechanical skills to do home renovation and construction jobs, helped us start over. I began to work in a special education class and completed my master's degree, which enabled me to earn more money. Eventually, by 2011 we finished working our way out of our financial hole. Though I encourage everyone to start businesses and take a chance to live your dreams financially, be aware that the global economy affects us, even in our own neighborhoods. Be aware of economic trends, look at changes, and be conservative with spending and credit as you use it to grow.

Don't Let Your Possessions Control You

The struggle to rebound from times of financial hardship helped us appreciate things more and strengthened our connections to each other. We know that the American Dream is to work hard and improve our level of living. It is right to take yourself to the next level to show your children the path of self-sufficiency and prosperity, but it is also important to teach them that money must be controlled and saved. Just as all behaviors are learned, so is the ability to train yourself to live within your means and to use discretion with your finances. Train your children to be aware of money and its ability to free you or enslave you.

Parents have the ability to control a child's appetite for material possessions. As a role model, you must exemplify the difference between purchasing something for necessity or for indulgence. We all need TVs, computers, and cars, among other things, but it is possible to be financially content while living within your means. If you are driven by the impulse to spend, spend, spend and get the latest "gleam and bling," then your children will adopt your obsession with material goods.

Media advertisement is the greatest challenge, as it molds the American consumers' minds, insisting that we buy the next great technology, clothes, shoes, or gimmick. We all receive self-satisfaction from buying items we want. This is acceptable until your need to impress becomes an obsession. We fall into the trap of "I'm not good enough unless I have that thing." You feel like less of a person when you do not have a certain type of tennis shoe or car. For many, it is a self-confidence issue, but self-confidence should be developed from within rather than from worldly possessions. As mentioned before, moms should instill confidence within their children as young as possible by developing inner discipline through talents and accomplishments.

When I was coming up, there was no such thing as designer tennis shoes or jeans. We did not have all the choices of today's young consumers. My grandma and mom bought for practicality because they wanted whatever they bought to last. They always had a ceiling price that limited their buying, and they enforced self-control when shopping. My mom always schooled me on how she came to the reason for her shopping choices. She taught me her budgeting techniques and explained why she bought this but not that. Once she selected the item and determined a comfort price, my only job was to pick a color. I was taught that buying should not be emotionally driven. She also taught me how to respect and take care of what I bought, because we lived solely on my father's monthly paycheck as a teacher. Lastly, I learned that if we could not afford it, then we needed to exercise patience until we could buy it later. This mantra of waiting until you can afford it is a hard obstacle to overcome, but the peace of mind that comes from financial security is priceless.

TEACH YOUR CHILDREN AND TEENS NOT TO BUY IMPULSIVELY

All children want things such as toys, clothes, and fun foods, but it is imperative that you do not develop the habit of buying impulsively or fall to your child's unnecessary demands. Children learn to beg and plead in stores when parents respond to their child's tantrums each time they shop together. Children learn how long it takes until their parents cave in. This is another internal-clock situation. The clock tells them about how long and how many screams it will take before Mom or Pop folds. Children tell themselves, "I must be loud, whine continuously, and bang or pull things. If they don't give in then I will cry louder and become more annoying until they need me to be quiet and give me what I want." However, spoiling your children with too many material things will lead to an expectation of getting new things all the time. Unfortunately, this behavior may continue throughout their teenage and adult years, which could cause major credit problems.

After experiencing this while we were trying to keep our heads afloat with our business, I realized that the credit card system is meant to trap you into many years of debt that typically leads to a twenty percent increase in your original ticket price, which is a waste of your money. As we struggled to pay back balances on ten different cards, I advised my children never to get caught in that type of race—the race where your opponent is debt and is always ten yards ahead of you. Teach your children about debt and warn them about how overextending credit through credit cards and loans can lead to losing everything that you have worked so hard to obtain. If you do not really need that thing, then do not get it. Or if you really want it, wait until you can afford it.

TEACH YOUR CHILDREN TO SAVE AND HOW TO SPEND MONEY

Although we had to sell our business, we had fifteen to twenty years of robust financial success, and to get to that point, we needed to save for many years. We live in a time when the latest and greatest becomes "old news" very quickly. My mother grew up during the Great Depression in the 1930s, and she often told me about her two pairs of shoes; she had one pair for church and one for school. These shoes would last until she outgrew them. She often repaired holes in her shoes with pieces of cardboard. In the '60s, a pair of Keds, church shoes, and one pair of school shoes were a sufficient supply for my young wardrobe.

Today, there are so many options for kids to wear, and the availability to shop by phone or internet makes spending much easier. When my children were all under the age of twelve, I would take them to shop. I would let them choose T-shirts or jeans. We shopped off season to hit the sales. I found that July and February were the best times to shop, as the stores were changing their inventory to make room for the next season. During our shopping time, we discussed how the value of one pair of expensive shoes could buy three tops and a pair of jeans. Additionally, I emphasized that the value of a dollar can go farther if you shop smart and with patience. The money we saved was stretched to buy accessories, such as earrings and belts, which could be shared. As they grew older, I resorted to getting them new clothes only for birthdays and Christmases.

Toys would also only be purchased at these times. In between the kids would sometimes make their own toys. I remember one hot summer day when the kids spread five black garbage bags across the lawn. We turned the hose on and had an instant "Slippidy Slide" for the whole afternoon. It destroyed the lawn with ten kids or so, including a couple of cousins, sliding face forward through the water. Our kids got strange looks from people passing by, but even they began to smile as they realized what was happening and recalled their own "Slippidy Slide" memories.

When my children became teens, I did not choose the style of clothes for their Christmas presents. My taste was not hip to teenage fashion, so several weeks before Christmas or a birthday, we would go out and shop together at the mall, and I would walk behind them as they window shopped and tried on clothes. They would discuss among themselves certain jackets, skirts, and blouses, and I would write down the item and the store. Later that week, I would go without them and pick up three presents for each.

There were always enough toys to share. One PlayStation was enough for all the kids. They seemed happy because they appreciated the few things they received. My girls would usually buy one or two expensive tops and then go to discount stores to buy jeans or accessories. Their outfits always looked great! They learned how to borrow each other's clothes and understood the respect it took to take care of others' property in order for the reciprocation to continue.

As time went on, my children went away to college. At one point we had five in college at the same time. This was also the time of our business woes, and even though their tuition and board were paid, we still had to pay for their airfare. Thus, one of our largest household expenses was purchasing round-trip plane tickets. I saved up and did not mind forking out four or five round trips each year, because December was a chance for everyone to see each other. Those were our best Christmases because it wasn't about material things, but rather about seeing, enjoying, and discussing the great things everyone had been up to while away.

Make Money the Old Fashioned Way—Earn It!

The respect of money is important. You can start teaching your children about the importance of the value of money as soon as they can count from one to ten. Let them know that nothing is free in life—you must earn and work for anything that is worth having. Get them a small piggy bank and have them save up for small purchases such as popsicles or even ice cream cones. As your child gets older, set small saving goals for them. Never give your children an allowance without making them actually work for it. I never encouraged allowances, because I wanted my children to realize they needed to help around the house regardless of whether or not they were being paid for it. In return for their service, I paid them for special jobs or treated them to eat during family outings, but general housework was not rewarded monetarily.

Use your common sense and know your child. You want to be fair and balanced about how you save and how your child spends money. If you do give an allowance, require your children to earn it by doing chores or having responsibilities. Some families have bank accounts or savings accounts. Learn to discuss finances with them. Counsel them on interest earned; investing their money is very important as they put money toward long-term plans. Please make sure to teach them about the disastrous rollercoaster of credit card debt before they leave for college. Help them to develop credit by buying an item on their credit card and paying back the balance before the close of the month in order to build their credit score. Finally, teach them to appreciate what items they have purchased. Help your children build self-confidence so they will be more responsible with their finances as they mature.

Teaching Your Child Time Management Skills

Taking time for granted is something those who are young are able to do. Young people have time on their side, and the furthest thing from their minds is the worriment of wasting time. It is truly important that you teach management skills by creating schedules, having access to clocks, utilizing calendars, and organizing their time to complete due dates for school projects. You, as the adult, must work on your own time management in order to help your child learn how to achieve more by using time more efficiently rather than wasting it. By second grade your child must be able to organize their time to be successful in life and achieve their goals. We will address Mommy time management in Section IV—The Empowerment of Mom.

Chapter 6

Teaching Your Children about Prayer and Faith

There is a reason why my children were successful in many of the things they attempted. They proceeded in their situations, whether good or bad, because they had a firm belief in God. No matter what religion you adhere to, you need to teach your children to direct their hopes, needs, and ambitions through a faithful practice of prayer. Whether once a day or weekly, prayer helps them to stay grounded in having a strong attitude toward challenges and a thankful heart. Connection with an energy greater than themselves may help them feel empowered and open to expressing their needs. To see the world around them as a glorious creation, and knowing they are part of that creation, gives a child a sense of belonging and optimism in their words and actions. Prayer also brings a chance to connect, a releasing of troubles, and a petition for direction. A relationship with God should begin young and develop through the years as day-to-day events occur. To pray is giving praise, being thankful, and asking for what you need. It gives hope and satisfaction to life so that your child feels happier, stable, and, thus, produces more.

Chapter 7

Teach Your Children to Develop Goals

Our family always talked to each other about goals—my goals, my husband's goals, and our children's goals. Expose your children to books of achievement that tell the stories of underdogs and the importance of striving against all odds. Show them how ordinary people can succeed by being resilient when dealing with problems, and teach them how to focus with determination. When they were younger, my children did not like to read; in fact, they hated reading. Since they were not natural book lovers, I took them to the library once in a while. We went to the library, and I would walk with them to the biography section and look for picture books, usually sports or political figures. When they found pictures of interest, we would read about the person. We found more pictures, and they eventually developed a desire to actually read about the person. Personalities such as Dr. Ben Carson, Muhammad Ali, Gayle Sayers, and Althea Gibson were examples of biographies they found interesting. These individuals were in sports or medicine, and my children could relate to them and so became more inquisitive. I sometimes would mentor and pick out books on types of musical artists and then rent their albums and play them while my kids were completing their homework.

At times we would sit down and watch documentaries about people who survived horrific events, people such as Shep Zitler or Eva Galler from the Holocaust or Hunter Bear from the Civil Rights era in the South. These people had experiences I could never have imagined, and their stories helped build knowledge of tenacity and courage. In reading about these people, their tales about mental focus during ups and downs and being on the edge of life helped my children to understand the power of the human spirit in the midst of turmoil.

As a family we were also blessed to have several people in our lives who I called "my angels." These people were positive role models for our children and were involved in their lives on a daily basis. My angels included neighbors, teachers, relatives, and coaches. They loved being around our large family and enjoyed being a part of our hustle-bustle lifestyle.

I guess there is a lot to say about big families and the total unpredicted reality of having so many children in one household. These friends would come over and help me by playing with the children while I finished some housework or took a much-needed break. From birthday celebrations to helping me with the kids when I had the flu, they would stay in our home and soak up the energy and joy of unexpected calamities that children get into around the house. Later in our children's lives, they had tennis mentors and those mentors were always there to help our children learn to improve their tennis abilities. They showed my children how to play within the game, how to change their strategies when necessary, and how to be positive when faced with an opponent's dishonesty and/or aggressive parents.

Life lessons come from mentors just as much as they come from parents. Mentors helped my children grow and develop their dreams from day to day. I strongly recommend that you help your children find someone to help mentor or coach them. Expose your children to accomplished people who will give them good advice. Mentors have their proper place and time within your child's life, though. Always communicate with the mentors and continue to monitor the relationship of trust between you, them, and your children.

Coaches, teachers, family members, and friends who have solid personalities and exhibit successful careers and reputations should be considered as your relay team. Take the time to sit down and talk to those who influence your children. I always took time to sit at courtside during practice and talk to our children's tennis coaches about my children's progress or about matches from the past weekend. Though they were busy coaching while we spoke, they would always stop to talk for a few minutes. Over the many years, these brief but intentional talks led to them becoming like family as we invited them over for graduations, parties, and birthdays. They were sincere and honest, yet firm in judgment about our children, and there was always mutual respect throughout the years. Through their coaches and Fred, the goal was always to play fair and well and to achieve college scholarships by working Saturday by Saturday, practice by practice, and hit by hit.

MENTORING GOALS AT HOME

As parents, you need to share interests and goals with your children. My husband and I always had goals in place. Some were more attainable than others. From wanting a house in the hills to being financially independent, we always shared our dreams with each other. We had a "dream book" that had pictures of our dream home. When our older children were small, they helped us construct this folder by cutting out magazine pictures for our future living room, bedrooms, or even the outdoor pool. Sometimes on the weekends we would cruise through Beverly Hills, Bel-Air, and View Park so that my children were exposed to different lifestyles. We drove to the poorer side of town as well. Every city has lower socio-economic areas, and you must never let your children forgo reality. As we drove through these areas, we talked about how life choices they might make could place them either uptown or downtown. I wanted them to realize we were blessed by God and able to hang on somewhere in the middle class.

Later, our children kept several wish books that contained photos, keepsakes, and diary entries of what they would like to accomplish, along with their tournament ribbons and trophies. It was influential for them to look at their siblings' trophies, ribbons, and newspaper clippings. This practice began as they watched their father maintain his collection of woodworking machine brochures and work toward his goal of having a large woodworking business. He kept brochures of every machine he wanted to purchase. He memorized every detail of the machines and would concentrate on saving money until he was able to buy them. He would study each product and then share the information with the kids and me. He told us the function of each machine and when he planned to purchase it.

Sometimes, when we would pile into the car and drive around Beverly Hills or Bel-Air looking at the mansions, there were constant shrieks from the back seat. "Oh, that's my house," or "That's where I'm going to live," or "Daddy, how much do you think that one cost?" followed by, "What kind of job do you need to get that house?" Little did they know that our field trips were very purposeful because they reinforced the idea of dreaming, which would lead to hope, which would lead to planning and action.

I always believed that hope was the eighth child in our family. Hope was always present on our children's faces. Later, when my children played tennis and the matches went brutally bad or when financial disaster hit, we always looked toward a brighter day. Hope in its smallest form is more powerful than the greatest mountain and can help you through the worst discouragement. That is why it is important to expose your children to the spiritual power of prayer.

Never discourage your children's ideas or interests. Every person is put on this earth for a reason. Everyone has talent; some are shining stars in the rough with intellectual abilities, while others have creative interests. It is often the parent's support or lack thereof that makes or breaks a child's effort. When my children had an idea, big or small, I would say, "Let's give it a shot," or "What is your plan?" or "How did you come up with that idea?" Sometimes, their siblings laughed at their brothers' or sisters' ideas, but Fred and I stopped the teasing right away. Talking with each other and discussing details of future plans lets your child know you are interested and believe in their dreams. If you appear interested, then you become their biggest cheerleader. If you seem disinterested, they will be less apt to pursue and will want to investigate other ideas that might not be as fulfilling. It is important that you commit a certain amount of time to discuss your child's progress with them.

Monetary support toward lessons will be necessary only if your child's interest seems to continue for a long period of time. It is also good to inform the rest of the family of everyone's activities, because you may have a network of friends and extended family that can help and advise, barter lessons, or teach in order to help them pursue their goals.

In addition, I also taught my children goals as I completed my teaching credentials and earned my Master's in Special Education. I was in class off and on for four years, and I let my kids know about every class I took. They witnessed me struggling at the computer, and they saw me studying nightly. Both Fred and I showed them timelines of how long things sometimes take. Exposure to short- and long-term successes kept everyone on board and interested. This caused a reciprocal effect, as our kids became cheerleaders for me and their father, especially me while I was completing my master's degree. Every so often they greeted me with a simple, "So how's it going, Mom?" or "Are you almost finished with your class?" They would taunt me sometimes by saying things like, "You're not gonna finish," "You can't hack it!" or "You haven't finished that paper yet? What's taking you so long?" But it was really their way of saying, "Keep going, Mom. You can do it." The encouragement was often needed, believe me, but in a way I was teaching them a very valuable lesson. If I could go to school while working and raising seven kids, then surely they could make their plans work too.

SUPPORTING YOUR CHILDREN'S GOALS

Supporting your children's goals is very important. Their accomplishments give them a purpose and an actualization of what they are capable of doing with their lives. To fulfill a goal is an amazing feeling, and navigating through the peaks and valleys makes us mentally stronger. I never expected to go for my master's degree, but our financial problems directed me to obtain the degree to improve our situation. You never know what events of life will pull out the best in you. It is through the harder situations that we are made stronger and wiser. Looking back, every day in our household was filled with challenges; yet, we were determined to follow a family routine. This is how we built our business, obtained college acceptances, and achieved scholarships.

Teach Tough Love while Reaching for the Goals

As our children worked on their goals, constructive criticism was real and necessary. For example, we always comforted our children after a tennis loss, but Fred was never too rosy when they lost the match. Constructive criticism in small doses invoked tears, but the message was always clear so that problems would be worked out the next day at practice. Being too hard causes resentment in children. Yelling *at* them and not talking *with* them will make a child turn away from you. They need to hear input, if necessary, but they must see you as a supportive mentor in order to receive that input well. Parents can be so passionate about their children and the goals they want their children to achieve that they sometimes run their children's interests into the ground as the child is pushed too hard and too fast. Your children only want to please you. So whatever happens, do not let the pursuit of goals get in the way of your relationship. It is important to set a schedule which will help to promote growth, a time for support, a time for fun, and a time for serious scrutiny when necessary. This next section shows how we ran our household and what it took to win our race.

PART III

PACE AND PUSH

Chapter 8

How Did Our Family Achieve Our Goals?

We Developed a Growth Mindset

> *"Remember that I have commanded you to be
> determined and confident. Do not be afraid
> or discouraged for I, the Lord Your God am with
> you wherever you go."*
>
> ~Joshua 1: 9

I must confess that achieving personal goals is a very difficult challenge for everyone. As a runner, my goal is simply to finish my workout without quitting. Goals can also be frustrating, as efforts to achieve them can be impacted by outside variables you cannot control. Our goals influence our daily growth. I believe that everyone has a reason to be on this earth. Pursuing a goal, whatever it may be, can make your life fulfilling and inspire others as well.

I have always pushed myself to accomplish goals in my life. Some goals were more attainable than others, but I could not imagine my life without pushing myself to achieve something that makes me a better person. When I finished at USC, I knew I wanted to be a teacher because I loved working with children. I have always enjoyed the innocence and energy children seem to naturally possess. I always found joy in helping, directing, and advising them. The glow in their eyes when they understand something for the first time or when they have that "aha" learning moment has always driven my interest.

I tried to observe better teachers and emulate them so I could be a better teacher. I visited classrooms that looked inviting, and interviewed teachers who had the most motivating lesson plans. I always brought my camera and pad to those special teachers whose students revisited them year after year to share old stories. Those teachers always had projects brewing and work covering the walls. I spent hours in some classrooms to soak up the ideas and knowledge of how to become a good teacher.

The race toward your goals begins with a plan, but your greatest challenge is to develop the resilience and flexibility necessary to change the pace and reroute your race if needed. When I was twelve, I saw Olga Korbut, the renowned Russian gymnast in the 1972 Olympics, dance her way into the world's hearts as she triumphantly astounded everyone with her original gymnastic moves. Despite a disastrous fall on the uneven bars, she later rebounded in the individual medal rounds and won gold medals for her beam and floor exercises. Her spirit and drive made her an automatic idol and celebrity around the world.

I was excited! I thought, if she could do it, so could I. At that moment I felt compelled to be an Olympic gymnast and become the first American to win an Olympic gold medal. I was enthusiastic and overly optimistic but determined. I could not be stopped as I looked for places in Los Angeles that taught gymnastics. I was thirteen and could not drive, so thank goodness for my mother, who saw my passion and found a YMCA about forty minutes away. It was about twenty minutes by bus from my high school, and sometimes, I took the bus after school three times a week. From that bus I then had to walk another half mile. At the Y, I worked out with girls and boys who had been practicing for years. I worked hard with no down time. I learned with ease the common tricks like cartwheels, rolls, etc.

Unfortunately, the more advanced classes with aerial rotations were difficult for my larger, teenage body to complete. I remained in the lower advanced classes longer than other kids because I could not execute certain tricks. I was older, and my body was bigger and taller, which made it difficult to jump high enough to complete the rotations. I would fall on my head, back, and butt. To my embarrassment, some of the other girls were cynical and teased me. My trials began to affect my confidence and determination as I slowly saw my dreams of being an Olympian fade.

Rather than quit, however, I decided to focus on completing smaller goals, and I started a team at my high school. This was more familiar ground, but I still frequented the YMCA to practice my stunts. It took me a year to successfully accomplish a back-hand spring and side aerial. Finally, I did it! During a practice session, while helping me complete my stunt, the coach told me he had not helped me rotate for the previous twenty back-hand-spring attempts. I was so overjoyed that I spent the next hour and a half doing the same trick over and over again. I shared my success with everyone: team members, my parents, my dog, other kids on the block, or whoever took the time to acknowledge me. I knew how hard it was to achieve that goal. I was in heaven, and no one could take that away from me.

It was a wonderful accomplishment, and I still tell my students that story. Although I never made it to the Olympics, diverting my goals with a little flexibility allowed me to prevail, despite a change of plan. If your plan does change, continue to push yourself, as each new door will open to even greater accomplishments.

It is so important to push toward a goal because it forms who you are. It guides your routines and influences the people you inevitably meet. I remember at my son's graduation from Howard University where Oprah Winfrey was the keynote speaker. As she addressed the graduates, she told them that when you find something you are passionate about, put your soul and energy toward it, then you will be successful and the money will come. She said that you must find something that makes your juices churn.

Before gymnastics, my mother got me involved in piano, ballet, and other activities that were time fillers but were not interesting to me. I never practiced because I did not want to, as I thought there were better things to do with my time. For example, I took piano lessons for six years but would only practice one or two days a week, usually the day before my required lesson. It was good to learn a musical instrument, but due to my lack of practice and discipline, my skills were very mediocre.

Pay attention to your children's interests, then nurture, encourage, and support their development within their chosen field. If you want to expose them to something such as a sport or skill, then push them to explore those things. Have them commit to something for at least two years instead of starting and stopping a new activity each year. Be consistent in being the vehicle that fuels their efforts so your child will understand and appreciate the feeling of victory. Build on their self-esteem as you travel through the peaks and valleys of your child's race.

Developing our Family's Business with Little Money

Building a business was my husband's idea when he left USC. In order to do that, we had to create a plan. We had little money, so we needed to start with a baseline plan to spend wisely and save soundly. To make ends meet, we had to exercise frugality with our finances as we watched, read, and asked questions to strategize and eventually come up with our own plan. It was all about making the smallest details count. Our monthly income was always the same, so we used this as a baseline. Fred brought home

$1,200 a month, $400 for rent, $400 for the machines, and $400 for utilities and food. For extra money, I provided childcare for family members. In order to save money, I breastfed each of our infants until they were ten months old. (Hats off to moms who are breastfeeding their babies while working. You are the eighth wonder of the world.) I even breastfed the twins at the same time when necessary. This was difficult but much easier than using bottles, especially at night. And I used cloth diapers instead of disposable diapers for four of our seven children. This was manageable until the twins were born and I lost the battle of keeping up with the poopy mess.

As our family grew, I cooked to help keep the grocery bill down. We often had casserole or soup with lots of beans, potatoes, rice, and bread. This filled up their tummies faster than light food. I bought vegetables such as greens, string beans, and green salad, which were less expensive yet filling. I cooked and calculated the servings to spread a meal for two days. Of course this changed as my children grew older. Daily tennis workouts and growth spurts resulted in larger appetites, but I always bought a lot of fruit to fill them up between meals. Fancy dinners were saved for holidays, and we really would cook and eat a lot on those days. When my kids came home from college, they anticipated a homemade meal. I couldn't believe the time it took a turkey to go from cooked and served on the table to a boney carcass; it was warp speed.

In addition to these savings, I made my baby food in a blender. I even attempted to follow in my mother's footsteps and tried to sew clothes for my kids, but this was not for me. Rather, I quickly found that hand-me-downs from close relatives and friends were equally as effective. I wish we'd had the internet back then because I would have loved to utilize Groupons.

I will admit that sometimes we were too frugal, putting off personal expenses in order to take care of the necessities of our business. Our machines allowed us to produce more quickly so we could complete orders monthly and open seasonal stores at malls to sell our gift items. Fred, Fred's business partner, Alex, and I traveled to wholesale shows and spent hours manning booths to sell our products. Yes, Solange, Kenny, and Melanie would travel with us, too, as we drove by van with our gift products.

Unfortunately, we put off large personal expenses to save as much as we could monthly. Our living room's design palette was our bed on the floor, Solange's crib, a second-hand pool table and a small black-and-white TV that was located under it. We did not use credit cards unless it was an emergency. For everything else, we saved and waited until our money matched the price. Issues within the business meant less decorative furniture for a few years. Although we kept out of financial debt by watching every dime, I did have some regrets as we put off purchases to compensate for the slow growth of our business. At times I felt envious of friends with no kids and their expensive lifestyles, but eventually, with a little patience, all of our needs were met, in addition to most of our wants.

Birth Control Blues: You Can't Box with God

Our plan was to not have kids until we were established; but there was no birth control method that seemed to work. I was unable to take the pill because of my low blood pressure. The doctors told me I could get a blood clot and risk a stroke due to a history of hypertension in my family. So we used all the other methods: diaphragms, condoms, jelly, and a combination of those, but pregnancies occurred anyway. Sometimes, we would use two methods at once while monitoring my ovulation calendar for fertile times, all to no avail. With all the preparation, it felt as if we were getting ready for a military offense maneuver.

Don't get me wrong, we both wanted kids, so there was no problem in having several. But after our fifth child, Fred and I agreed that birth control was not working for us. We agreed that Fred should get a vasectomy. Well, that did not work either. When Michelle was fifteen months old, I went in for a routine check-up and discovered I was pregnant again. During the ultrasound, the nurse saw two heads. I told her, "Turn off the machine, because it must be broken. That is impossible!"

She said, "I'm sorry, Mrs. Brown, but you're going to have twins."

I lay there stunned, thinking that someone was playing a joke on me. But when no one yelled, "Surprise!" I began to ponder the reality of having seven children. I cried as I drove to my husband's business. Prior to even giving him the news, he saw my teary eyes and knew there was more than one this time. He fell face down to the floor with his hands cupping his face. It was always in his thoughts that we might have twins because they ran in both sides of the families. I myself was a twin and the chances were very high that someone in our extended family would have twins, and he felt it could be us. But with Fred's vasectomy, we thought we had dodged the bullet.

Getting pregnant with twins was not met with enthusiasm from either one of us. It was most difficult for me because I had to manage this big group, and my plans of helping with the business would be further out of reach. I felt a mixture of overwhelming apprehension and anger. There were a few times when I threw my fist up at the heavens for overriding Fred's surgery. This was the ultimate derailment of our plans. After a lot of introspection, some fussing to God, and conversations with Fred, I was finally able to accept this surprise. Clearly, the Good Lord wanted all seven of them here. After the twins were born in 1994, I decided to get a tubal ligation.

From the outside looking in, I know people thought our family looked like a crazy menagerie. Yet many also admired how we kept things going and were able to keep advancing. I believe in fate, but having seven children under the age of eleven made things complicated and tiring. Even so, we continued our race, diverted yet determined. I remember being pregnant with the twins when we finally bought a 10,000-square-foot building for our business. We had been saving for that moment for years. It was a beautiful brick building with skylights and was big enough to house all the machines, an office, all of our wood, and up to twenty workers. It was a proud moment for Fred and his parents, who were beaming as we took photos on opening day, standing with our five kids and me pregnant as could be with two more on the way. Though it seemed crazy to some, things were working out. Both the business and the family were growing. We had achieved much in a fifteen-year period, even though it seemed to be at a very slow pace.

Looking back, we both agree that life was fun, simple, and a lot of work for both Fred and me. During the earlier years of the business, when we only had Solange and Kenneth, it was always nice when Fred came home. He would arrive home after working two jobs at about 9:30 p.m. He would play with the kids and we would all talk as he ate his warmed-up dinner. He told us about his accomplishments for the day, and I told him what the kids had done. Since the kids were not yet in school, we could stay up late, and Fred would playfully wrestle and joke with them. They would be so wound up that when the "Tonight Show" came on, they would mimic Ed McMahan, shouting, "HEEEERE'S JOHNNY!"

I loved those first few years together. We did not have a lot and nothing was fancy, but we had fun! During the day, before they were old enough to go to school, the kids and I would play under the pool table when other neighborhood kids and cousins came by. Although staying at home to raise your kids can be a challenge financially, I enjoyed playing, reading, and doing simple things like sitting outside in the yard, going to the library, or just watching them play. Looking back, I believe the idea of hope for a better tomorrow kept us humble yet optimistic and, most importantly, complete.

Chapter 9

Seven Kids Under the Age of Eleven

When Solange became an older sister at age two, I taught her to help me take care of her brother. I wanted her to become involved in our day-to-day activities with him. I made her fetch diapers, bottles, and wipes, and even had her sing to Kenneth to occupy or soothe him. I wanted her to get a sense of the responsibility and patience required to be a good older sister. When Kenny was born, he needed to stay in the hospital's intensive care unit due to a harsh intestinal tract infection. He stayed in the hospital for four weeks and came home below weight, so it was important that he be constantly monitored.

I wanted my two kids to be close from a young age as they worked and played together. I told Solange that, as the older sister, she was a teacher to her brother, but I also told her she had to be patient while I tended to his needs. Through playing together, she also learned to share. They shared the same toys and even shared the same bedroom. I had them do everything together. I did this because I wanted to raise children who were not selfish and self-centered. Sharing taught them how to compromise, solve problems, and learn to deal with each other. Settling problems, innovation of play, and just learning to be patient with one another should start as a child. I truly believe that those who share as children probably make better students, spouses, and problem solvers in life.

As more of my children were born, it was important that we establish a daily routine. Our families' lifestyle was loud and spontaneous with babies crying, billiard balls down the toilet, and a missing hamster, yet routine was the basis of our day. Everyone interacted yet understood that the day's routine made things predictable. When the kids were young, their daily routine would include watching "Sesame Street," "Mr. Roger's Neighborhood" and "Reading Rainbow" together in the morning. (As a child I grew up with TV role models such as Engineer Bill and Captain Kangaroo.) These shows presented adult figures in situations that required reasoning while teaching basic human values to solve situational problems within a thirty-minute span. Of course, these programs were fantasy, but they captured the interest of children.

Teaching social values such as teamwork, helping your neighbor, hard work, and ethics training are universal childhood problems that were often addressed with puppets, cartoons, or personalities my children learned to love. Today, you can purchase whole series of these old TV shows, many of which are still entertaining. These shows also helped my children develop good verbal skills as, later during the day, Solange and Kenny would mimic or sing what they had seen. After the shows ended, they had to earn playtime by completing chores such as making their beds. We often went on walks or visited places together because I wanted them to see the world at an early age. The more they experienced, the more they would learn, reflect, and express themselves.

Car Time is the New Family Time

As more of our children were born, I found that I needed to drive a lot more. So I kept a separate to-do list on the refrigerator for all the places I usually shopped: a list for the mall department stores, a list for the hardware store, and a list for the grocery store.

Keep your lists at a location that makes it easy for your family to contribute on a daily basis. Then, when the list gets full and you get paid, you will use less time and gas running around.

Together as a group in a car is a great time to catch up with each other. Furthermore, if at all possible, try to have dinner with your family. The traditional family dinner has become an endangered species in this day and age. With everyone on different schedules and fast food readily accessible; garnering the time and attendance of the entire family is difficult. It is much easier to join together when your children are younger. Try to keep this habit consistent so it will remain in later years when your children become teenagers.

Some families have game night or try to make sure Sundays are spent together, watching a football game or other group activity. I hope in the coming years that I will be able to eat a Sunday meal at least once a month with most of my children who are now married or who do not have Sunday job responsibilities.

It is healthy for the family to bond and connect when experiences are shared. Advice or correction to life's situations during discussions helps to nurture family relationships. Slight comical anecdotes helped our family enlighten siblings about school, dreams, and tennis situations. Later, when my children became teenagers and they traveled back and forth to practice and/or tournaments, car time was used to express frustrations and laughter as the tensions of the matches were released. If your family drives a lot, extend the trip and take the long way home. One of my pet peeves is to see everyone in a car looking at video games or popping in earphones as soon as they get in the car.

Families have limited time together; so do not spend it mentally isolated from each other playing with electronics. The automobile is the modern dinner table. Start the conversation by telling everyone what you have done that day. Put away the cell phones, IPods and headphones; these things rip apart family time. Listen and learn about each other. Learn about football plays, subjects at school, projects, practices, and lessons learned. Discuss what other families are doing, but do not make this a time of gossip. Discuss important activities or others' family accomplishments. Your children may find new interests as they discuss other' experiences, extracurricular activities, or opportunities that might advance their own interests. Two of my daughters were able to participate in internships at hospitals because we talked to other families who shared job information. It is healthy competition to "keep up with the Joneses"—as long as it is done in a positive manner.

LURE THEM IN FOR SUNDAY DINNER

One way to secure family time is to create a well-prepared meal to lure them in. You can cook or order food and disguise it by putting it in a fancy bowl. Make it look like you went to a lot of trouble. Start while your children are young. This will be much harder if you start when your children are teenagers. Have patience and spark conversations by discussing something that is in the news. Communal time allows everyone to be aware of each other's interests and personalities. If all else fails, and they do not eat together, you can lay down the law and threaten them with no dessert (oh my!). Or you can have Dessert Sunday; that might entice them as well. After the third or fourth time, it will become more natural and help to solidify a genuine family bond.

OUR DAILY ROUTINE WITH SEVEN KIDS

Once the school years started, our routine changed as our seven children's needs and destinations changed. Our weekday usually started at 5:30 a.m. I woke up early to have some alone time before the kids woke up and the day's hustle began. I needed silence to mentally prepare for each day. My "me time" consisted of different things over the years, from riding a stationary bike for fifteen minutes, to studying and learning to speak Spanish for forty minutes each day, to reading the Bible for guidance. Sometimes, I would hate getting out of bed so early, but later, I was glad I had done something for myself. At 6:15 a.m. I would prepare a big pot of oatmeal for everyone. It was important that my children and husband went to school or work with a full stomach. As mentioned before, on Saturdays we would have dry box cereal that the kids prepared themselves. We would go through four boxes of cereal and one gallon of milk so that everyone could make two bowls each. They were so excited to have this ritual, so they would sit together, eat cereal, and watch cartoons, allowing Fred and me to sleep in. On Sunday after church, we had a big breakfast with pancakes or French toast, along with eggs and grits.

However, getting back to our weekday routine, as the oatmeal was cooking, I lined up bread on the table for sandwiches. Since lunchmeat was too expensive and salty, our menu varied from peanut butter and jelly, to cream cheese and jelly, to a fried egg or tuna sandwiches. I would form an assembly lunch line. Next to each sandwich was a piece of fruit or small heap of baby carrots and usually something more fun like chips or a snack bar. Boxed fruit drinks were too expensive after times got tight, so a thermos of juice or milk sufficed. Each grouping of food was ready for packing by the kids. If they did not get up in time to pack it, then it would stay there. It was their responsibility to pack their lunches themselves. When my children were older, and I was working late or attending school, they would make their sandwiches the previous night.

When they were younger, I ironed their clothes, but as they grew older, they were responsible for preparing their own uniforms.

Uniforms were great because they diminished the mental anxiety surrounding what to wear the next day. My children washed their shirts nightly and wore their pants for two days before washing them again. September was the most expensive month as we bought four to seven sets of uniforms. The rest of the year was easy, save for growth spurts or busted knees that resulted in repeat visits to the uniform store. Wearing uniforms alleviated problems of borrowing and switching clothes back and forth, which could lead to fussing among siblings.

There was no television or radio on school mornings because it was too distracting. My children did not need anything to make them late; they already moved slowly enough, as most kids do. Since we had one bathroom, everyone had a designated bathroom time.

My biggest feat when my children were younger was backpack preparation. I guess they inherited that from my undersupplied diaper bag church days. Always check to see that homework has been put in the backpack, even after they claim to have put it in. This helps avoid lectures at teacher-parent conferences regarding missed assignments and make-up work. Middle school- and high school-age students are not immune from backpack prep. Over the years I found other students' sweaters, smashed bananas, and even a bag with a dead fish that Chris had won for a poster contest.

Most teachers supply a syllabus with assignments or a check list, so put this info on the refrigerator. The refrigerator is the best place to post schedules, reminders, and notes because it is the center of the house. Another good place to write notes and reminders with a dry erase marker is the bathroom mirror. This is the other main hub of the house. Make sure the backpacks are ready at the door the night before. As my children grew older, these practices helped them become more organized and prepared. If they become good with the small things then they will be more responsible with the bigger things later. Don't forget, Mom, to tell your children that you love them and give them a kiss before they leave for school. If they don't like to be kissed, then blow them a kiss, because those six hours at school can be tough at times.

Days are always more productive if mornings go well. Find a routine that gets everyone organized and prepared as much as possible the night before. The mornings will run smoothly and your children will benefit.

After School with My Brood

My home routine was pretty predictable before and after school. The middle hours of the day—such as toddler naptime or when everyone was playing outside—needed to be more flexible As my babysitting responsibilities decreased, I wanted to keep busy with activities that challenged me during the day. Being at home when my children were young was a blessing, but at times I needed something to keep my mind churning. Housework can be boring, and I didn't want to become a "Desperate Housewife." Being a restless person, I was always working on something extra, as long as I could work at home.

My strong Christian beliefs inspired me to create and organize church fellowships. I planned them over the phone between the little ones' naps. When I wasn't networking, I practiced the piano or worked on business taxes with the mother of Fred's partner, Alex. After school was all about my children! During the mid-years, when three of our children were in elementary school and we had four at home, I would pick up the school kids, come home, snack, and get right to work. Homework was spread across the table, and I catered to whoever needed the most help. Everyone had to be busy reading or studying. Later, after the twins were born, the older children had to help the younger ones read, color, or do something so that everyone joined in. Even at two years old, I introduced picture books to encourage reading. We would work for two hours and I would read with everyone individually. I started dinner early while the kids finished their homework. Seldom did they stop and play before dinner at around 7 p.m. Yes, there were constant phone calls and visitors coming by, but we tried to stay on track. Fred would make it home about 7 as well.

At this point in our financial journey, he was operating his business full time. When the kids were young, everyone ate at a large table in the kitchen. Starting about 7:45 p.m., the younger kids would alternate bath times. With only one bathroom in our household, we were cramped, but we never had fights or arguments. There was no lock on the door, so everyone had to knock and be patient. The only time we had problems would be after everyone returned home from a long outing and had to go "pee-pee" at the same time. The boys would go at the same time and race to see who could finish the fastest or who had the longest pee-pee stream. Believe me, I had to clean around that toilet all the time! In the evenings, once homework or piano was completed, they would then play in their bedrooms.

Until they were older, Solange, Kenny, and Melanie, didn't have televisions in their bedroom, only a large communal television in the living room. The kids learned to share and used their imagination rather than be entertained by a television during their free time. They worked at crafts or played games that encouraged thinking skills. Dolls, action figures, small cars, and playhouses made my kids interact. I did not allow video games except on Friday evenings or Saturdays.

After the twins became toddlers, Fred constructed a large thirty-foot, three-level, wooden play apparatus that had swings, a tire, and slides. This was a lifesaver because my kids had something to do rather than be in the house all the time. It was safe, and other kids from the neighborhood often joined in the fun. This was like having a park in our yard, and it kept my kids active and busy on the weekends.

My children shared the responsibility of cleaning around the house. At the age of five, I allowed them to assist me with dishes. I would wash and my helper would stand on a chair as I handed them dishes to put in the drainer. We never purchased a dishwasher in all those years of rearing our children because I wanted each child to learn how to help during the day. I kept track of who did dishes by writing each child's initials on a calendar as they completed their responsibility. As each child reached the age of five, they joined the alternating dish duty once a week. Some nights we didn't get everything done, but I was never one to force a perfect kitchen. Washing dishes and putting them away was good enough, as I preferred to spend time with the kids and Fred.

We had an older home with two bedrooms and a full bathroom. We also converted our small den into a third bedroom. There were bunk beds in each room, and after the twins outgrew their cribs, everyone had to double up. We had three girls in one room and four boys in the other. They enjoyed the closeness, the chance to play, share toys, and use their imagination. On weekends, all seven children would pull their blankets onto the living room floor and watch Nickelodeon until 10:00 p.m. When their favorite TV programs were finished, they often slept on the living room floor like a giant slumber party, finally falling asleep about 12 a.m. They loved it!

OUR ACTIVITIES

Like all parents, we wanted our children to explore their talents and interests, so we began to look for after-school activities. We also had to consider our number of children and how expensive extra activities would be. On Saturdays, Solange and Kenny took piano lessons from my brother-in law. Eventually, when Kenny turned five, he began T-ball twice a week, and Fred became an assistant coach with his childhood friend Virgil. It was great that close family and friends helped us. Virgil would watch our sons until Fred got off work and joined them. Much later, when Chris and the twins reached school age, they joined the T-ball team too.

Summers, since school was not in session, meant even more running around, as we wanted everyone to keep busy. Over the summers we packed in everything from T-ball to piano to gymnastics. During the week, everyone took swimming lessons at the neighborhood pool. It was very important that all of our children be able to swim. All of our children spent at least three summers taking lessons. I wanted them to be capable of swimming in case they went to the beach or pool parties with others. After a few hours at the park pool, we would go home, eat lunch, then read or study for two hours. Some days, we went to the library. I wanted to maintain their reading levels during the summer. Although they did not like this time of the day, it was required and it gave them a chance to rest. During some summers, we took gymnastic classes twice a week at the Hollywood YMCA. We took my nieces to the gym classes in exchange or barter for my children getting piano lessons from their uncle. Solange and Kenny continued with piano and participated in recitals.

Our station wagon was always packed and moving. When we were stopped at an intersection waiting for the light to change, we would sometimes notice the occupants in the next car counting the number of children in our car. Once, someone stopped me to ask the name of my daycare center. Their jaw dropped when I told them that everyone in the car belonged to me.

During the long days of summer, we would go on an outing once or twice a month. We also have a friend, Javona, who let our family use her pool while she was at work. Anything cheap, from the beach on weekends to going to the train store, local aquarium, or my sister's house sixty miles away was simple but fun. We were a small party wherever we went. It was common that, when friends were giving a birthday party, they would only invite our family and a few of their relatives. When we showed up with seven kids, I would hear, "The Browns are here, now the party can start!"

Chapter 10

The Tennis Years

Now, I must back up a few years in time to when the twins and Michelle were very young (around the church potty-crisis time). In 1993, tennis became an important part of our summers. My husband had begun playing tennis daily at the Rancho Cienega Tennis Stadium near our home after work. After running back and forth with so many summer activities, he and I realized it was becoming hard to continue in so many different directions: gymnastics, art, baseball, swimming, and piano. At the same time, Kenny was beginning to struggle academically in school. Reading did not come easy for him. Even though he tried very hard, he continued to have academic problems. We decided to get him tested at UCLA and found that he had a visual perception problem that impacted the way he processed letters, words, and numbers.

As my husband began to look down the road toward high school and college, he realized that admission requirements had become more stringent and competitive since more international students were applying to higher-level U.S. schools. Having a high grade point average was not good enough anymore. School admission boards looked for a more rounded student with a balance of academics, athletics, and community involvement. Fred could see that he needed to focus more time on Kenny and apply his energy wisely.

Through Kenny's T-ball experience, Fred recognized that Kenny was good at sports, so he decided to develop Kenny's ability as a student athlete. Kenny was naturally a quick runner, agile, and a hard worker. Fred, who was a high school running back himself, knew what it took to excel in sports. He knew that sports would increase Kenny's options of being accepted to better high schools. Above all, Fred wanted Kenny to be eligible for college scholarships, and he found that tennis increased the probability of Kenny earning an athletic scholarship rather than competing in the more popular sports of football and basketball.

In 1993, Kenny and his father began playing tennis for two to three hours after school. Kenny had a lesson once a week at the Venus and Serena Williams Tennis Academy in Los Angeles. Fred would play with him, reinforcing all he learned as a player himself. Since my husband owned his own business, he shifted his regular ten-hour workday to begin at 6 a.m. and end at 3 p.m. After a few years of training, Kenny began to win matches. Competing helped his self-esteem as he began to win. Later, Fred recognized that tennis could be the way to help all of our kids and began to focus his energy toward obtaining possible college scholarships for each of them as well.

For several years now, Fred's business had been doing well, as his line of wood products were being sold in many art gift shops across the country. This was about the time that Fred and Alex bought the manufacturing building and increased our production by expanding the company to include more employees. This allowed me to stay home with Michelle and the twins. The other children continued at private elementary and high schools. I took care of home, school, and studies, while Fred took care of our business and tennis activities.

Terry Chambers, our tennis instructor at the program, coached each child. After three years of working with Kenneth, Melanie began to take lessons. Solange was not included in tennis because she was already thirteen and considered too old to begin. She seemed to like softball at school and also participated as a junior lifeguard at the park pool.

As mentioned before, Melanie was easygoing with a friendly personality. She was the dancer of the family, so she was naturally poised and had an ability to extend with great balance. This gave her great tennis form with good shot consistency. Unfortunately, she initially lacked the desire and competitiveness that tennis requires; thus, it took her longer to advance. Christopher began a year after Melanie. Chris was energetic and liked competition. With different personalities, my husband and our coach, Terry, had to use different teaching methods within a daily, three-hour routine of exercise to develop each child's skill.

During the early years of tennis, Solange attended a parochial high school that was thirty minutes away from our house. I shared carpool duties after school, so I had to complete several drop-off points for Solange's friends and then pick up our children from their elementary school by 3:15. I would meet Fred at the courts, drop off Kenneth, and then take the rest home for homework. When Kenneth began high school, he took the bus to the courts. When school tuition prices increased, and the twins were old enough, I decided to take a teaching position at my children's school as the seventh grade teacher in 1996. I enrolled the twins in the school's pre-kindergarten for free, as the school honored the family rate. It did not hurt that I was a teacher there. This was convenient, as we arrived together for school and left together at 3:20 p.m., grabbed a snack at home and changed clothes before Fred picked up Melanie and Chris, and off they went to the 4:00 practice.

As tennis advanced, weekends became very hectic for everyone. Saturdays were spent running to tennis tournaments about an hour away in Orange County. Major tournaments had several age levels competing at three or four locations simultaneously. Upon winning, our kids were sometimes required to switch locations within the hour to play their next match. We were one of few African-American families at these tournaments, let alone being the largest. Everyone recognized us and knew when the Browns arrived. Needless to say, the weekends were crazy as Sunday competitions became the norm. Gone were the days when church members saved a row for us in church. Since we were always on the road, we would go to church the day before or just read the Bible when possible.

As we continued to go to tournaments, people became intrigued by our family and extended a helping hand to support us with our tennis goals. Mentoring programs, such as College Match, which supported student athletes with scholarship opportunities, tutors, and college outreach, approached us. Recruiters from colleges came to tournaments to watch our kids compete and talk to my husband. Competition was heated, as every tournament could change your ranking and affect your ability to receive scholarships. Organizations donated tennis shoes and racquets, while the Venus and Serena Tennis Academy paid the kids' tournament fees and offered additional assistance when needed. Our race was running smoothly, but every race has its bumps.

Financial Distress during the Tennis Years
When a Storm Hits, Keep Your Pace

Kenneth, Melanie, and Chris went to three different high schools. Each child had different academic abilities and Kenneth's, which was an all-boys school and Melanie's, which was an all-girls school, offered tennis teams. Michelle, who had begun playing when she turned six, was more competitive and aggressive. Hence, after a successful record in city, statewide, and national tennis tournaments, she was offered a full, four-year scholarship to one of Los Angeles's most prestigious preparatory high schools, the Marlborough School for Girls. This opportunity was given to her because her sister, Melanie, had played against the Marlborough team and soundly beat every girl. Their coach quickly went to Melanie and asked if she had any sisters. So Michelle, who had good grades, was one of four accepted from a pool of 130 applicants. By 2002, our five eldest children, except Solange, were playing for their high school teams and competing in the California Junior Circuit on weekends.

My husband's business began to have challenges as he invested in a second business. With the success of our first business and ample manufacturing experience, we began to design custom car wheel rims and custom packages to detail cars. Although we started off strong, we soon began to experience the pre-recession years, beginning in 2003. Smaller American companies began losing economic ground to government-subsidized companies based in China that were larger and could mass produce with lower overhead expenses. Previously manufactured goods and machinery parts from smaller American companies were being out-sourced for cheaper-priced, high-volume products that were shipped at a lower bottom-line cost to larger American companies. High insurance costs, compensation requirements, and taxes caused many large companies to seek cheaper overhead overseas. Suppliers closing up shop, underpriced competitors, design theft, and pre-recession economics drained both of our businesses as one struggled to support the other. This caused Fred to split his attention between business survival and tennis.

Hard Times, Good Hearts

In 2004, the twins began tennis at age ten, which is considered a late start. As tennis continued every day, the problems outside tennis were frightening. My husband was trying to balance two businesses and deal with the kids. Unlike the woodworking art business, auto accessories required fast-paced production. The demand for competitive designs, lack of suppliers, and unforeseen problems became overwhelming. The unfortunate economic domino effect also occurred with other local businesses as well. When a business supplier or client went bankrupt and failed to supply materials for our company, we fell behind in getting our own orders out. Unfortunately, we learned how ruthless business people can be when in survival mode. Design patent infringement and bad advice led to continued problems. In hindsight, I believe we were too trusting in accepting business advice as we applied for city business loan incentives.

As mentioned before, to curb personal expenses we decided to stop renting our home and move in with my mom since we had been paying her mortgage for some time. Our personal finances were tied to the business, and we had to struggle for five years to keep our home. I began to work for the public school system and took classes at night and on weekends to complete my Master's in Special Education. Creditors were calling and we had to sell our building to cover the cost of loans. Fred and Alex worked for eight years, trying to work things out. We closed and sold our businesses in 2008 after the stock market crashed and the worldwide recession began. It was so disheartening as we watched twenty years of effort and sacrifice come to an end.

During this time, I worked an additional shift as an adult-night-school teacher for two years. Fred continued to sell wheel items through the internet for two more years. Without my presence at home during the evenings, the youngest, now in their mid-teens, had to adapt and manage for themselves, helped only by my mom. I believe our many years of frugality made the years 2003 to 2010 manageable. These were the tightest years. I worried the most at each Christmas because, for so many years there had always been so much under the tree on Christmas mornings. Fortunately, family helped on occasion, and as the twins became teens and our older children began to leave for college, the burden lessened. It was a necessary change but my family understood and accepted the minimal. Some say that your character is demonstrated during times of adversity. Although our situation was tough, my family showed character throughout those years of financial distress.

With everything going on, we still kept an extremely tight schedule, as I continued to teach and pick up the twins from school. Solange and Kenneth were now away at college. Michelle, Melanie, and Chris took the bus from all over parts of Los Angeles to get to tennis practice by 4:00 p.m. sharp. The lessons lasted until 7:00, and they all arrived home at 7:15 to eat from the crockpot and study until midnight. There were some years that I would attend class or teach adult school and arrive home and try to read with the twins, only to fall asleep. I believe we kept strong because of our faith. The stress of all of the outside factors was calmed by our spirituality and faith as church continued to be a part of our routine. Attending Sunday services as often as we could and participating with choir practice on Fridays kept us going. Understanding the positivity of God in our lives helped us all stay focused.

The many people we had interacted with recognized we needed help and continued to work with our children in tennis and at school. The children continued tennis with the help of Charles

Thomas and Terry, who had now played with our children for several years. These were "my angels" who understood hard work and who helped my husband mentor and keep track of the kids and their progress. They were truly family, and I give acknowledgement to them for helping us with our children's tennis successes.

During those difficult years, my husband would be late getting to the court and sometimes wasn't able to come at all. Charles and Terry would be there and not only taught my children tennis but modeled the importance of helping others and encouraged growth by communal support and discipline despite what was going on around them. Depending on the availability of classes for my master's degree, I would teach during the day then, semester to semester, teach at night to help pay our business loans down. As mentioned before, when I was teaching night school, I would drop off the kids at the court by 4 p.m. and zoom to work; it was Charles or Terry who often dropped off the kids after practice.

The best part of these later practices was the camaraderie between our kids as they came from three different buses from different parts of Los Angeles. You could set your watch on the appearance of our clan showing up at the tennis courts. Except for the twins, they were all at different schools, so when they finally got together at practice, they were glad to see each other and would start practice with chuckles and bantering among themselves.

It was unofficially understood that the same four courts were to be cleared by 4 p.m. because the Browns were coming. There were many older players, some retirees, and regulars who played at the courts daily who were respectful of our children's consistent practice schedule. They would save the courts for us just like those who saved our church pew on Sundays.

As time went on, our children were spread across five courts, and Fred, Terry, and Charles rotated among them. Fred tried to work with each child daily. Although business pulled at him, he was there almost every day, and when he wasn't, our kids never missed a beat since their mentors, Terry and Charles, were there to work with them. Terry and Charles were familiar with each child's strengths and needs. It was a five-ring-circus, mental puzzle that my husband had to juggle every day, yet it was orchestrated, as each child knew their set routine, depending on needs demonstrated at the prior weekend's tournament.

All the tennis regulars at the park, especially the veteran players, knew us and admired the continuation of the Black tennis legacy at the park. Our kids always let everyone know how they had done at tournaments. My children took time to discuss matches from the beginning to the end with details that were comical at times. This kept everyone at the park involved with our family. And we began to depend upon them all to help support our routine.

The years of our children being respectful, playing and talking with these adults, gave the regulars at the park a sense of mentorship toward our children. It was common to hear their raspy voices giving verbal inputs and quick-check comments that kept my family on their toes. "Hey, you all need to work on your backhand stroke," or, "You kids are looking pretty good today." Some of our kids had special nicknames that were affectionate ways of promoting a family atmosphere. You do tend to do better if you know someone is watching you. Fred was friendly with all the regulars, and everyone knew he was serious about his plans for his kids. When Fred and I were in hustle mode and missed some practices, it was comforting to know that our kids were not on the streets after school but practicing with their extended family of sorts.

The court folks liked us and assumed mentorship roles with the kids. They became part of our lives and were always informed about what our kids were doing in school. They even knew the results of weekly tests and grades. They would give advice to my children about listening to their parents, staying out of trouble, and moving in the right direction. They would express compliments to my husband that our children were always nice and respectable. But one of the best outcomes of working daily at the park was the exposure to retired professionals, such as lawyers, doctors, and community representatives, who took time to teach to my kids about school, hard work, and character building. Other members at the tennis park began to know about our family and know there was a true consistency and purpose to their practice.

This got the attention of other families who came to the courts. Some of them shared carpooling to the courts, and our children made good friends. As more children came to participate, they practiced with ours and they, too, began to win and acquire interest from colleges. In 2003, our family received the Southern California Tennis Association Family of the Year Award. This garnered even more interest toward our family. After being published in an annual tennis publication, scholarships, college connections, and internships became available. Christopher won the United States Tennis Association Sportsmanship Award. Even the beloved "Cookie Man of Rancho Park," who sold cookies around the park for a living, would take from his own earnings to supply my kids with ice cold water on hot days. These stories of common decency were inspiring to me and kept me going.

On weekends my children would play tennis while I ran at the adjacent track stadium. There was a balance of Browns everywhere at the park. The park regulars at the track knew me, and they knew I had tennis players at the tennis stadium about 500 yards away.

The regulars at the tennis stadium knew me as "the kids' Mom," but in reality I believe they thought of themselves as extended moms and dads. For over twenty years, they watched our family grow up. Our lives were their lives. By looking at our family, they were a part of our victories, losses, and learning experiences.

Community Giving Back and Receiving

Over the years, summertime at the Venus and Serena Tennis Program would bring more students to the park, and a common-core group of young tennis players in the View Park area of Los Angeles was formed. This summer program also included a tutorial service instructed by brothers Richard and Fred Williams, the program directors, who challenged the students with SAT exam preparation by using math and vocabulary games. For many years, my children benefited from the program. As a result, Kenneth, Chris, and Melanie would take time to play with other kids at the park who wanted to learn tennis. This was also a good experience for my children because it gave them the opportunity to mentor aspiring players. Later, the program provided jobs for Michelle, Melanie, Nicholas, and Matthew in both high school and college.

The tennis program flourished as students, including our children, began to win consistently at various tournaments, producing highly ranked state- and national-level tennis players. Kenneth was ranked among the top twenty players in his age division in Southern California and traveled to national competitions. At home we worked with him academically, and he became sought after by college coaches. Tennis coaches from across the nation began to check out the tennis program. Our own children were given an opportunity to interact with representatives from sports equipment companies that donated gear to the Williams' program participants.

During Kenneth's senior year of high school, he was ranked #7 in Southern California. He won most valuable player in his high school division and was recruited by Howard University with a full, four-year scholarship. As he played for the team, he ranked #1 along the East Coast college circuit. He was the team captain and continued to assist in coaching for the Howard University team for several years.

As mentioned, Melanie formed both varsity and junior varsity tennis teams at her high school, St. Mary's Academy. She was the team captain and taught her team techniques and strategies. She won Most Valuable Player in the Sunshine League. She had always wanted to be a nurse, so with a full, four-year athletic scholarship, she attended Prairie View A & M in Texas. She captained the tennis team there for four years and helped lead the team to the finals of the South Western Athletic Conference Division for four years. She completed her degree in psychology and minored in pre-nursing and pre-biology. She earned her bachelor's degree and then attended Texas A & M, Corpus Christi, for her post-graduate work in nursing. She worked as a surgical nurse and has achieved her master's degree as a psychological nurse practitioner.

During Christopher's senior year in high school, he was ranked #27 in Southern California and accepted a four-year athletic scholarship to Howard University. He was the team captain for three years and graduated with a Bachelor's in Communication. He is currently working as a nurse specialist for the Veterans Administration.

Michelle earned a four-year academic scholarship to Georgetown and later transferred to Howard University to pursue biology, where she also received an academic and athletic four-year scholarship. She was the team captain of the tennis team for three years and won Player of the Year for the Mid-Eastern Athletic Conference Division. She has recently completed her Doctorate of Dental Surgery at the University of Southern California's Ostrow School of Dentistry and is working as a general dentist.

Finally, my twins, Nicholas and Matthew, received seventy-five percent athletic scholarships and graduated from Virginia State University. They both played for the tennis team and were both named Player of the Year in consecutive years. Both majored in biology. Nicholas has earned his bachelor's degree and plans to pursue his doctoral degree in physical therapy. Matthew has been accepted to the USC School of Dentistry, the same school where Michelle became a dentist. He plans to become an oral surgeon.

I completed my three years of schooling at the California State University Dominguez Hills Master's Program in Special Education and Administration Certification. Later, I earned my National Board Certification as a teacher. My husband continues to work in construction and design. We are currently working with our oldest daughter, who earned her real estate license. We have purchased our first income property and plan on working together as a family to purchase more together as an investment group.

Michelle, Nicholas, Matthew and Fred at one of many tennis tournaments.

PART IV

THE EMPOWERMENT OF MOM

Chapter 11

Empower the Epiphany

As parents, we put an enormous amount of stress on ourselves. We know we must do our normal daily routine. Unfortunately, this daily grind continues past our standard eight-hour work day. Often, we push the clock and ourselves, both physically and mentally, as we complete afternoon and evening routines. Parents often focus so much on their children that they lose focus of themselves. Due to our children's needs, we get up early, go to bed late, and drive many miles for their activities. We want them to do great, yet we run ourselves into the ground helping them. As they excel with their academics and extracurricular activities, the importance of our own well-being is pushed to the side. However, it is just as important that you, as a great parent, nurture yourself in order to be strong and productive for your family.

With today's squeeze of the recession, some parents may find themselves needing two jobs just to make ends meet. Generally, a household needs more than one income for a family to feel comfortable. Unfortunately, the workplace has become more demanding as companies consolidate and lay off established workers, which further strains the workplace. This also results in less job opportunities for our next generation.

As parents, the competitiveness of achieving the American Dream for our children includes attending the best schools and programs in order for them to compete in the job-placement battle when they reach adulthood. We want the best schools and education for our children, not just for them to compete but to shine above others. So consequently, we work harder and longer to afford the best neighborhoods, including a productive and safe school for our children for their optimal growth experience.

The push for excellence as the new global economy creates vast competition with large companies looking across the globe for job applicants is now occurring. The world is smaller, and the amount of technology to produce more efficient workplaces requires higher problem-solving and thinking skills. In addition, some parents feel the need to keep up with the Joneses, as television and the internet promote the latest material possessions or "must-haves" and trends. Now add a daily commute, school meetings, and homework—which, depending on the teacher, can take hours to complete—and you have a recipe for a tired and stressed-out parent. The extra activities, sports, and lessons could give your child an extra competitive edge, but it can be grueling. Just as in running a race, one can only go as fast as ability and training allows. As humans, we all have limitations within our given twenty-four hours, and it vitally important to take time to take care of ourselves, both physically and emotionally.

Physical Well-Being

Stress is a parent's greatest foe. The stress of your daily routine impacts your mental and physical balance as you try to complete your to-do list. There is something so powerful about young parents who have the will and spirit to push the clock and make every moment count. But remember, the spirit is driven by the mind, and that is part of your physical being.

We all have only twenty-four hours in each day, so when making a schedule, it is important to know our limits as well as our ability to balance ourselves for our own happiness.

Know Your Body's Needs

There is no clear answer to what each person should do for the well-being of their own mind and soul. Finding something that fulfills you and nourishes you comes with experience and introspection. Whatever your mojo, it is essential that you work it into your daily, weekly, or, at least, monthly schedule. Whether it is a pottery class or book club, one should desire to achieve proficiency through learning something new and challenging.

You must push the stress out of your body as often as possible so that you can produce well. The building of stress in the body will eventually affect your heart, muscles, and blood pressure. Find an outlet! At times of high stress at work, I would close my eyes at lunch and play soothing music. Many people walk during breaks or exercise at a nearby gym before going home. At home you must also develop an escape route to help you cope when things get too mentally challenging. When my children were young, it seemed that the only word I heard was "Mommy, Mommy, Mommy." I would go into the bathroom and take a relaxing bath or escape and sit alone on my porch just to have some peace and quiet. Once I finished, I felt refreshed and energized. Only then, and with a little prayer, was I able to deal with all the "mommies, mommies."

I advise ten to fifteen minutes of solo time a day to help maintain your sanity. As the house manager, you make many of the decisions, and you need time to refresh yourself so you can deal with your children wisely. It is important that you give a signal that you need time or space so you do not blow up on anyone. Have a place of escape when you need to distance yourself from everyone and take a needed pause. Sometimes, my children, my husband, and I would be in the middle of a busy evening, and

I would be preparing for the following day's school lesson. The combination of lesson preparation, coping with seven kids, homework, and chore coordination sometimes became overwhelming to me. I could feel my back tense and my teeth starting to grit. I knew I needed to get away or someone was going to be a victim of my wrath. I did not want to model such behavior, so I would take some time for myself and let Fred take over for a few moments or even a couple of hours. Of course, I would not leave everyone hanging, but throughout my years as a mom, I found outlets, such as a temporary walk in another room, playing my piano, or just jogging.

DRINK WATER, DRINK WATER, DRINK WATER

Many have asked me over my lifetime how I keep my skin smooth and young looking as I've grown older, especially while having seven kids. Much of it is due to genetics; my mom and grandparents have naturally young-looking skin. But I can recommend the most essential thing: drinking water. It hydrates your body to work well. It helps moisten the joints and encourages easy digestion. Slow bowel movements lead to waste building up in your body. I found that bowel issues made me feel slow and less energetic. But the biggest benefit that drinking water gives is good-looking skin. When I drank water, my face seemed smoother and tighter. Drinking a lot of soda and malts gave me small pimples and made my skin look ashy.

The problem with water is that it is boring and heavy to the stomach. There are so many other interesting things to drink that are sweet and fizzy. I found that drinking two full glasses three times a day was enough to feel and look good. In order to do this, I had to schedule a phone alarm to remind myself to drink water daily during weekends and, especially, while on vacation.

A schedule of discipline for me created a routine that my body accepted. As mentioned before, I wake up early to give myself private time. Now that my kids are older, I read Bible scriptures in the morning, which helps me focus on self-discipline so that I can establish a spiritual purpose for exercising good health. On occasion this helped me avoid certain foods I knew my body didn't need. As years passed, I noticed that my body would become thirsty at the same time every day. Being a teacher demands that I am on my feet, talking most of the day, so I need water to keep my engine moving. Sugary drinks leave me thirstier and tired. Drinking water refreshes you without bringing the highs and lows of sugary drinks. Remember to enjoy yourself by eating and drinking to your delight, but I strongly suggest that you schedule water breaks to get through your day better.

MOVE, MOVE, MOVE

In retrospect, as a mom I should have slept more, but there was always work to be done, whether it be with my kids, my husband, or my job. In light of my responsibilities, my running balanced me and helped me maintain stability, both physically and mentally. When your mind is happy, your body follows along. Your mind is the X factor in determining your self-achievement. It can also be your worst enemy if you begin to doubt yourself. A lack of confidence in your ability to do your best or try new things is a wall your mind creates. *I'm too old. I'm not smart enough. The task is too great. People like me don't usually achieve in those areas of life.*

As I grew older and a little wiser, I finally stopped saying those things to myself. I realized that I wasted a lot of time and energy due to a lack of self-confidence. By the time I was forty-two, and my youngest kids were turning ten, I began to run at the track in the evenings during summers. I would run a lap, then walk, and then run again. This simple chance to get away from my routine was exciting. My running would help me reach small successes every week. I wasn't always fast, but I finished. Achieving my goals built my self-esteem and confidence, which helped me in other aspects of my life.

While I was running, I could clear my head and sort out the issues that kept playing around in my mind. Regrets about the past or stuff that crowded my mind would not go away unless I exhausted myself with running and focused on finishing those three miles. It was also a time for me to work on my goals. I would develop short incremental goals and challenge myself to accomplish them.

I sometimes had difficulty completing my run. Regardless of whether I had eaten too much or if I was tired, I always tried my best to run at least two days a week. Running served three purposes for me: the ability to get exercise, feed my spiritual mind, and create my own personal freedom. It gave me a sense of control, as I had this time for myself rather than everyone else. It was a grind at times, but I felt good accomplishing something—so good that for the last twenty years I have returned to the same track again and again.

So find a physical activity that will move you both spiritually and physically. From something as simple as walking with a friend to mountain climbing, starting small with tiny steps will cause you to reach your best potential and feel great!

My Goal is...

Every woman needs personal goals, a goal that makes you feel victorious and self-confident, something that does not involve children or a spouse. As you achieve, you begin to believe that no obstacle is too big to attempt. You have more energy, feel good, and want to try new things. In my youth I had low self-esteem. Due to my diverse cultural background, which is a mix of African-American, Native American, Caribbean, and French, I was considered by many as different or exotic. Due to the way I looked, I always had attention and opportunities. People treated me differently. I realized I had been given a silver spoon long before I was eight years old. My looks always brought me more attention and opportunities than those around me. Consequently, I was often the teacher's pet. Throughout my school years, I would do naughty things like the other kids but always got away with it. I was popular for no reason other than my looks. I didn't have to try as hard as the other kids to join groups or teams. Everyone was my friend because it was the popular thing to do at my elementary school.

The problem with this micro-stardom was that it bred animosity among my friends, especially in middle and high school. Girls became jealous of the boys' attention toward me. Criticism from classmates increased every time I tried something new. My years of egocentrism made it hard to accept people teasing or being critical of me. I began to flounder and feel embarrassed. Yet older people who didn't know me still let me be a celebrity when I walked in any room. As time went on, I decided to go down the easy path of fitting in where the least effort was required. It was easier for me to be accepted as the pretty girl if I stayed within my comfort zone, not pushing or trying new things.

More problems came when I went to college and it was time for me to prove myself. I soon found there were plenty of other attractive people around and that vanity did not go very far. I found myself struggling with completing tasks, keeping myself on pace to compete with others, and dealing with defeat when things did not go well. Except for limited success with my gymnastics,

I found myself quitting things I tried because I did not want to experience failure.

At one point I was interested in going into medicine, but that idea fell by the wayside; I perceived myself as being too inadequate in math and science to compete with other students. I thought of acting or modeling, but in that highly competitive world at that time there were few opportunities for African-Americans, which caused me to not pursue that either. In a nutshell, I simply did not have enough resilience to face failure. I remember auditioning for a modeling job and hearing an agent look at my pictures and say, "If we're going to get a Black, then we need one that actually looks Black."

This lack of acceptance outside of my general surroundings was new to me. I had never experienced people being so harsh to me. The other would-be models at cattle calls intimidated me. I did not know how to cope with these new problems, so I avoided failure by eluding challenge.

With medicine and modeling pushed to the side, I earned my teaching credentials at USC and put my sights on teaching at the elementary level. While waiting for a job to come up, I continued to do general office work, but I always wondered what would have happened if I had pushed myself to pursue my original interests.

Later, my husband helped me to understand the art of disciplining myself toward a goal. After we got married and started a family, I was pushed to make daily decisions on my own that would help my family succeed. Each successful decision built confidence. Vanity cannot run a household. I had to depend on my own judgment to manage a functional home. I began to do great things with my kids and excelled as a woman, mother, and wife. As time went by, I realized I was quite good at what I did. I cooked, cleaned, worked, and managed a home better than others I knew, and still, I was able to commit time to my children's achievements. I was always making time for my family but then realized I had little for myself. This led to exhaustive days with little time left for rest. Running track and retraining myself in piano gave me a release without impacting everyone else's routines.

Running or learning music techniques is not easy, but it took my mind away from my regular routine. Maybe the run was a little slow, and maybe the song had lots of mistakes, but that was the challenge I needed. I did not need anyone to be my "yes man" because I was my own cheerleader. Confidence brought happiness that gave me more energy, and that energy was carried into my home life. Having outside goals also helped me develop patience.

Before establishing my own interests and setting goals, I did not have the mental endurance to finish things. I lacked patience because I never dealt with challenges long enough to understand that success comes in stages. When you work at something with tenacity, you develop patience, and eventually, you will see progress. Yes, there are ups and downs, but anything great is worth working for. Accomplishing short-term goals that will be the foundation for your overall goal is like watching a flower bloom. You do not notice the day-to-day change, yet you look up one day and find a beautiful flower that you have nourished.

Adversity will make you wiser and develop your skills. After each step you are a little stronger, a little more precise, and a bit closer toward your goals. This is where patience is acknowledged, and the victory of change is much more rewarding. So find your passion and work toward it; once you make your mark, keep going. No one can take that good feeling from you, and your family will reap the benefits of that energy.

Spiritual Energy—Get It from the Source

I am a firm believer that every person has a spirit. Most refer to it as your soul. Scientists and psychologists cannot qualitatively or quantitatively define it, but it drives our behavior. It is the energy that empowers us. Positive energy helps you feel good and gives you a charge to get up, improve, produce, and do. I believe this energy comes from a higher source than our own souls. I call that source of energy God. As a teacher I know that science books claim that energy never disappears but rather changes into different states or directions. Subsequently, I believe everyone has the ability to tap into this primary source or energy of God. My belief is that God is energy and that He created us and continues to transfer His energy through us every day. How we use that energy is up to us.

We can empower ourselves by opening ourselves up to the source of God through prayer, meditation, or reflection. We must take time to stop, quietly listen, and pray to receive insight and motivation on how to direct our given energy. Every mom should take time to reignite and renew the energy that God gives. Taking time to be quiet in a calm setting is a blessing most women miss because we are constantly moving in everyone else's directions. Moms are the driving force in every family. We are the organizers, the overseers, the ones who push everyone in the family. Your spouse and your children need you for guidance and to provide security and comfort. But if you do not have peace of mind, everything and everyone around you will reflect the chaos and tension occurring within you. When you are balanced, your family will be balanced too. They will become stronger as they see you utilizing your God-given energy.

Using this energy the wrong way is easy to do. With so much going on in our lives, we rush around so much that we rarely pause to enjoy the experience of raising our children. Energy can be easily transferred into a negative direction such as stress eating, self-pity, or constant thoughts of jealousy or unhappiness. It is imperative to keep your energy flowing in the right direction. We all have a purpose in our lives. Be flexible and creative by examining, meditating, planning, and being patient. You will see your own personal flower bloom and those around you will bloom as well.

Being Grateful is the Best Kind of Rejuvenation

As mentioned before, getting away for a few moments to move, relax, or divert myself helped me physically to reboot myself emotionally, but you must also renew yourself spiritually by quietly listening to God. For me that place was my front porch. It was a small porch, but I would shut the door behind me and sit on the stoop and let the sun hit my face. I would take several deep breaths and try to relax my body. I could always feel the tension inside me go away as I stretched my neck and shoulders. I would then take a few moments to thank God and acknowledge His blessings in my life.

We forget how many good things there are in our lives. Although things can be dysfunctional at times, our health and our family are what make our lives different and unique. Just thinking about these things can rejuvenate you. You can exercise thankfulness by expressing gratitude. Understand that your circumstances could be better or worse, but you should be thankful anyway. Things in your life may not have turned out the way you wanted, but continue to give thanks and push forward. Being quiet helps you to enjoy the natural peace inside you. Take the time to smell the flowers, feel the breeze, or listen to the birds because these things come from God. These techniques have been practiced by many figures throughout history.

A time to relax, meditate, and calmly reflect are holistic ways to make yourself healthier. We must take time away from cell phones, television programs, and noise to experience these clear thoughts. Sometimes on that porch I would just be calm, other times I received ideas, or I received guidance on important decisions I had to make. Feelings of emotion, anger, frustration, or asking God for forgiveness would occur during that time. My family knew to leave me alone for those ten minutes or so once or twice a month. I definitely had crying moments every now and then. It was always part of my repair.

After those times of meditation, I wrote down whatever had come to my mind so I wouldn't forget the new insight. It didn't always change the things around me, but it helped me to prepare, understand, and face those things with a stronger frame of mind and a wiser outlook. So find a time and a place, and respect that time so it becomes a chance for you to connect and repair. To steer away from the negative and reroute yourself to what God wants for you is essential to your well-being. Once your body and soul are in check, facing the world's surprises becomes much easier. Making time for me has made an extreme difference in my life. Nourishing my body and soul has made my family grow as a unit, and I hope it can do the same for yours.

Chapter 12

Family Time Management

The frantic feeling that there is not enough time to get every-thing done occurs about three times a day: morning, noon, and night. With work, children, chores, and a spouse, you may feel like the runner who hears the starting gun go off and sees the other runners take off, leaving you behind. As a young mom or even an experienced mom, juggling too much can leave you stressed. You begin to misplace things, forget dates, and you may get irritable because you feel tired and strung out.

I remember when my children were younger and we were running from appointments to tutoring sessions to tennis matches. Our usual Sunday morning routine was to get to mass. Well, this one Sunday was particularly stressful, as our sixteen-month-old twins were walking—usually in different directions—and while I worked to corral the twins, my hope was that our other kids would not trash their outfits before it was time to walk out the door. Even though Fred was helpful, we were outnumbered.

As usual our entire family walked into church late. As I mentioned before, there was always a pew strategically saved for us. That Sunday my mind was flooded with things, and I was probably thinking of all the things on my to-do list for the coming week. As I sat down on the wooden pew, I did something only an overly stressed and busy mom could possibly do—I absentmind-edly reached across the front of my body toward my shoulder as if I were reaching for my seatbelt. As I realized that I was in church and not in a car, I concluded that I had hit an all-time low.

When you drive so much back and forth from place to place, always thinking of the next thing to do or the next place to go, the seatbelt reach is a natural reflex. I realized that my routine had taken over. I felt like I was in the episode of my favorite television show, "I Love Lucy," when she was working at a chocolate factory. She was positioned at the factory conveyor belt to wrap chocolates into papers. As each chocolate passed on the belt, she was supposed to pick it up and wrap it. She was contently working until the supervisor sped up the belt. The chocolates came so fast that she could not keep up and they began falling on the floor. Overwhelmed, she compensated by corralling the multitude of chocolates and placing them in her hat or hiding them in her bosom.

That is how I had begun to feel. I was compensating for things going too fast. I ran late to class, so I had to catch up on lectures later at home, which caused me to delay correcting homework from my own students, which would back up report cards to that one weekend which was intended for resting. Modeling this to my children showed a lack of organization. It resulted in wasted time and making excuses for being late. I told myself there had to be a better way and that I needed to model efficiency to my children so they wouldn't be late, messy, or unproductive. My wonderful porch moments and runs at the track helped me to put things into perspective.

DETERMINE THE NORMS IN YOUR HOME

Part of what stresses moms the most is that dreaded housework monster, you know, that monster which confronts you every day. As the organizer of the family, you must step back and determine how to make your family function without going crazy trying to maintain everything. Troubleshoot your home so it can function even when you aren't present. Here is some advice to curb "the crazies:"

1. If your home is large enough, designate a family area where your children are to keep their toys.

2. If you lack space, designate a playtime and play space so your children learn to put their toys away daily, especially on weekends when your routine is unpredictable due to the possibility of visitors stopping by.

3. Have a place, such as a big plastic container or lots of shelving, where children are to put things. Write each child's name on this designated space so they know it is a special place for their things.

4. Decide what needs to change in your home. Ask yourself questions as you clean: Do I need to organize my home or organize myself more? Do I save too many things? What items need to be thrown out? Can I consolidate and store items to reduce clutter? Answer these questions and act. Take one area at a time and get some organization advice from magazines and design websites.

5. Have your children put away their things as early as age two. If they know where they took the object from, then they should be able to put it back. It creates less clutter and is easier to clean up.

6. Create stipulations or norms for your children within their routine so that chores must be completed before any fun stuff like TV, outings, or video games can occur.

To encourage clean up, I created a competition between the boys and girls in my home to see who had the neatest bedroom by bedtime. There was no prize for the winner except an extra kiss and hug as I tucked them in. The next day it was always hilarious to find extra toys and bundled up clothes hurriedly pushed under the bed or in a closet to quickly finish the competition the previous night. Although the spontaneity and unpredictability of children can make motherhood fun, establish the norms to make your household run as smoothly as possible to help you with your busy life.

Mom, You Must Organize Your Time Too!

Scheduling is the best way to not overextend ourselves. As mentioned before, we women take on everyone's needs. We do everything from chauffeuring children around town to counseling our children through teenage break-ups. With only twenty-four hours in each day, we must prioritize our time and not take on more than we can handle.

You need to break down your days and weeks. Plan with your spouse, family, and friends who help you, and discuss with them in depth what their designated responsibilities are. Remember, people get distracted. You can say something to someone, but they may have their mind on something else, and the message may not sink in. You do not want your child waiting in the dark because in-laws were not clear on their pick-up time or schedule. Organization necessitates a plan; take time to sit down and make a weekly plan in order to use your time and your family's time more wisely. Be flexible and always use a pencil when planning.

Organize your life by prioritizing your time. When doing this, divide your busy life into three parts: "Have To Do," "Should Do," and "Want To Do." First, compile your "Have To" tasks. These include your work, driving time, and sleeping for at least six to seven hours each day. That leaves you with about five hours for additional activities, as I mentioned before. Those five extra hours should be allocated toward the "Should Do" list, which includes such tasks as chores, dinner, or events like after-school activities, studying, and the extra stuff involving your children. Plan and prioritize those five hours daily at the beginning of the week or month and stick to it. Your child's success in school should be a top priority on your "Should Do" list. Block out time for reading, library time, or homework.

Combining activities and allocating responsibilities will determine how successful you are as the administrator of your home. Start writing out your schedule and leave yourself timeslots for down time to spend with your kids. As you plan the "Should Do" tasks, remember to include individual time for yourself and time for your spouse. Be reasonable and balanced so that your "Should Do" items are possible and do not take away from your family or quality time from yourself. Organize your household where things are designated to others, such as babysitters, so that home life flows normally when you are away. Whoever is helping you needs to know the family routine and stick with it, or you may come home to find more on your plate than when you left.

As time went on, I learned through my own bad experiences of wasting time that planning ahead is the way to go. Eventually, order became my routine, which was very important to me in achieving my own outside goals as well. I would get up early and carry my list in my notebook and place it on my desk so I had everything ready for my students, my family, and myself. I found that my schedule minimized frustrations of last-minute decision making.

I have always hated making decisions in haste. If I rushed a situation, then I would often find myself doing damage control all day. With seven kids, I found there was always something happening: a bloody nose, slammed finger, or a last-minute request to run to the store and pick up poster board for a project that was due the following day. Since the rest of my day was organized, I had more time to assess the situation more calmly. The following are several scheduling tips that will help you with your "Should Do" list.

For Weekdays:

1. Make a schedule at the same time every night to prepare for the next day. Include work, after-school activities and house/family time.

2. Enforce the schedule. Compliment your kids if things flow well.

3. Respect your schedule. If you do not practice it, nobody else will.

4. Be flexible. Things happen. But write it down as things change or you may forget. Have a hardcopy phone book and carry a small calendar. This may be "old school," but it does work. Remember, we do lose cell phones sometimes.

5. Know when your children have school reports and projects due the coming week so you can gauge your prep and assistance time.

6. Make your spouse and children clean up after themselves; i.e., clear the table, put dishes in dishwasher or at least in the sink, put clothes away, and put bathroom stuff away.

7. Get to bed in order to allow yourself six to seven hours of sleep—spouse time not included. This can be tough to plan but it is very important! If you have a significant other, get to bed earlier for intimacy so proper attention—romance— is given to each other.

For the Weekend: Every weekend will be different so a new schedule should be done before each Friday.

1. Respect others' free weekend time. By knowing others' schedules, you will eliminate conflict regarding pick-up times, use of car, or events to attend, as well as your own personal time.

2. Leave yourself ample time to come and go. Traffic can have a significant impact on travel time, so know alternate routes.

3. Try to plan your meals for the week. This will cut down on those extra trips to the store. I did not prepare big meals for the weekends. Sandwiches or a big breakfast on Sunday was good enough. As your children get older, have them prepare simple meals like spaghetti or tacos so you can have time for your "Should Do" items.

4. Don't forget to plan something for yourself so the weekend does not whiz by without some form of personal indulgence.

5. Utilize technology. Computers are a great tool for making your life more efficient. Make a schedule on your phone, with ring reminders to help keep you on track. Computers can help you with many things from balancing your budget to turning on your coffee in the morning.

Keeping the House Clean

The "Should Do" items, if scheduled well, can be the X factor where moms can really gain time for themselves. So you need to train yourself and your kids to anticipate completing each item on the list in case there is a change of schedule or unexpected company.

Our home seemed warm and active yet cluttered and jumbled. I would feel somewhat embarrassed, as visitors might be greeted by numerous socks and shoes and empty drink boxes on the porch. Then as they walked in, they had to avoid the wave of toys across our living room floor: toy cars, half-dressed dolls, Legos, rearranged furniture everywhere, and makeshift tents made from sheets and towels draped across chairs. Jokingly, as I uneasily looked around, I would attempt to explain the wreck to my guest. "Um, this is not Art Deco, it's 'Art Wreckco.'" As a young mom, I did not realize that my kids could pick up their own toys before they went to bed. Unfortunately, I enabled them by taking *my* time to pick up *their* toys, which caused them to develop lazy and sloppy habits. The time was wasted completing the "Should Do" list when I could have been doing something from my "Want To Do" list—like taking a relaxing bath. So you must include training the trainer as well as those you are training.

Delegating responsibilities should be at the top of your "Should Do" list. Teach your family to support you. Gone are the days where women do all the housework. Work allocation should be expected and discussed with your family and support persons. You want to be clear and not wishy-washy in your requests so there is no confusion as to who is supposed to do what. This will ensure that your children will grow up to be responsible and able to do housework with good work ethic.

"No One in This House Has a Maid!"

When your children reach preteen years, teach them how to pick up after themselves on a daily basis. Unless your children anticipate winning the lottery or expect to become professional athletes, they will probably not employ a full-time maid. Never let them eat in their rooms, because this is a bad habit and will follow them into adulthood. Teach them how to clean and scrub their home the correct way. You should make them do light cleaning such as vacuuming, dusting, mopping, and bathroom cleaning on a regular basis and heavy cleaning twice a year that includes wiping fingerprints off the walls, cleaning cabinets, and scrubbing off grease behind and under the stove.

We had a cluttered home, but it was always clean. So model your cleaning and then watch them clean the same area. Teach them to clean thoroughly and efficiently and fuss if it is not done well. As young adults, teach them, and they will improve as they get older. Doing the small things well improves work ethic and will empower them toward better self-efficacy, task completion, and responsibility.

Lastly, try to redo the décor of your home from time to time to keep things fresh and inspiring. The least expensive way to do that is to paint and rearrange the furniture. When times were tight and we had to limit summer excursions, we would distract our children by doing low-budget renovations. I had my kids paint their own bedrooms so they would understand how to be handy in their own homes. Have your kids help pick a color and discuss how the furniture will be placed. Your children will feel proud knowing they helped their home look nice.

Every summer we had a house project in which we all contributed. It was actually fun, as everyone had something to do. Make your children work together on small projects as a team so they are not overwhelmed at first. You don't want to feel like Cinderella's wicked stepmother, so compliment them as you teach them. Then make a big deal when the job is done right. Brag on them to the other siblings so they will see how excited and proud you are of them. Compliment their teamwork; working together will help decrease sibling rivalry. After consistent work and good behavior without complaining, reward your kids. Treat them or do something special after a hard day of work. As I mentioned before, positive reinforcement goes a long way, so from treats to allowance—if they earn it—then let it flow!

I sometimes embarrassed my kids by over complimenting their nice rooms. Be silly! Take a picture of the Clean Room of the Week! Put it on the refrigerator next to the chores. Don't worry, I did my part on Saturdays with a good once-over of the high traffic areas, but your children and you will benefit from good and productive work, and you will all have more time for those "Want To Do" items.

Finally, solicit scheduling advice from women around you who have similar lives and responsibilities to yours. Don't look at someone who has one child if you have three. Don't try to implement the same schedule as someone who lives closer to their job. It's all about relevance to your situation. Remember, it is your household and you are the leader.

Mom, Don't Take on Too Much Stuff!

Life is about choices, even for Mom. You need to prioritize the extra things that you may want to do. Now, once you have trained yourself and your family to self-regulate their habits, don't fill up your newfound time with more "Should Do" tasks. Children do not have to attend a multitude of activities to develop their abilities. Limit the activities, and your children will still get into a good college–believe me! Simply make sure the activities you choose allow your child to excel through hard work and good work ethic. Take time and do simple things with your children.

As a teacher I know that good schools are important, but the time after school between the hours of 6 and 8 p.m. can make or break whether or not a child is successful in school. Cherish the time when you can sit down and read with your children and learn something new. Discuss things that you find on the internet that coincide with what your child is learning at school. Take time to enjoy motherhood, because it's easy to miss the scenery if the merry-go-round is moving too fast.

LOVE YOURSELF

Above all, your "Should Do" tasks should include loving yourself—which is a "Want To Do." As moms we can get caught up in the tornado of our family. Always remember to get an annual, physical check-up, because you need to know about your own health. Do not delay! You owe it to yourself to remain healthy, especially as you get older.

Go shopping at least once a month. You want to look good. You should look pretty. I think this was a problem for me. I wish I had spent more money on clothes. I thought that saving a penny was worth it. I would always spend money on my children, so it was not until my girls hit their teen years that I realized how far out in left field I was. My daughter Michelle would say, "Look good, feel good, do good." I believe I needed a coach, and I started looking at how other women dressed. I also found that discount stores and thrift shops were great ways to get a lot for a little.

To feel pretty and sexy is something every woman should experience. Always believe you are worth it. Budget every month or so for a shopping day and try new styles that accentuate your good qualities. Be modest, but do not go frumpy. Remember, your spouse is looking!

Chapter 13

Stay in Love

Marriage a sacred bond; it is reflected in every religion and culture. Unfortunately, many do not treat it as seriously as they should. In our household the sacred vow of marriage is very important. At the time of writing this book, my husband and I have been married for thirty-five years.

Spend time with your spouse. Although it is rare these days, I know it is possible. All marriages and relationships are different, so for me to sit and preach to you about what works and does not work is misguided. But the bottom line is that you need to give each other time and respect. You must spend time and communicate about your day-to-day lives, no matter how mundane daily activities may become. Every day, Fred and I ask about each other's day and outline what we did. Although we have the same conversations every day, it keeps us connected. My husband and I discuss everything from school, business, the kids, tennis, fixing things around the house, and usually money issues. Even when things were very bad and we were trying to keep our business and our home, small talk was encouraging to us. Sometimes, suggestions caused debate, but in talking every day we grew closer together. Helpful advice, a continuation from yesterday's conversation, or a chance to let off the steam from the day was typical.

It was important for us to talk for several minutes to each other alone in our room when he came home from tennis with the kids. It also allowed the kids to eat and catch up on their own lives. It was our transition time to regroup and switch gears. In the earlier years of our marriage, we would wait until the kids were in bed and sleeping so that we had some quiet time to ourselves. When possible, ask family or friends to babysit so you and your spouse can catch a movie or take a walk together. When we went out, we tried not to talk about kids, cartoons, or our children's activities, even though the conversation would inevitably end up on the kids.

Marriage or a relationship means that your discussions may be argumentative at times. These arguments can be passionate because you want to get your point across. Both sides want to win, but each person must practice tolerance toward the other and, sometimes, sacrifice to find common ground. Sometimes, the stress is caused by other reasons that build up over time. Perhaps, you and your mate need a break away from your regular routine. I remember many times when I would take the kids to a tennis tournament on a weekend to help give Fred a break from the intensity of the matches. Over the years I learned to read the small signals he sent when he was tired or overly preoccupied. Sometimes, he would do the same for me, giving me time to feel better and be more able to cope. Remember to be considerate and mutually beneficial to your spouse. After our business closed I became the one who brought in more money. In a recession it is typical for women to make more money, but it is important not to become condescending because of shifting financial dynamics.

Sooner or later, one of you might get ill and you might become a caregiver sooner than you think. Hence, it's important to be considerate of each other as partners through all that life will throw at you. Your partner is an extension of you. You are a tag team. Know how and when to help each other. Your spirit needs that constant balance of a spouse or friend. Your emotions are more in balance if your relationship is healthy.

Within your home the way you talk to each other in front of the children also impacts how they will deal with their own spouses. Many parents want to involve the children in arguments, making their children think they are part of the problem. So try not to nag your spouse, especially in front of the kids. Nagging can turn off your spouse, and the children will see the worst in both of you. Give your spouse or partner compliments in front of your children. They will enjoy the love you show, even though they may say that it is "gross." Surprise your spouse with treats, flowers, or an unexpected gift. Once, I surprised my husband by kidnapping him from work. We went to the movies and spent the night at a nice hotel. Romance is very important, so keep things fresh and spontaneous. Nothing kills a marriage more than taking your spouse for granted. It makes the marriage boring and you will become emotionally sluggish.

Over the many years we have been together, I often needed to focus on the things I loved most about my husband to avoid dwelling on the negative situations going on around us. You need to think back and remember the things that brought you close when you first met. For me, I have always loved my husband's comical side. Even though he seems quiet to many, with me he can be silly and full of fun. I am the more serious one, so we balance each other out. No matter what is going on, I can rely on that side of Fred.

Another thing I love is my husband's hands. Being a craftsman, his hands are scarred and rough but very skilled and strong. He can fix anything, and I love to see him work. So when things seem stale, I always look at my husband's hands. When we go walking, and I always just hold his hand. We currently run at the beach on Saturday mornings. We are older now, so we must encourage each other through the moans and groans. He runs beside me for four miles, and then we sit on the beach together afterwards and talk about our aches and pains. It may not be romantic, but the time spent going through the same experience and building upon each other is priceless.

Find that thing that opens your heart about your spouse. It will help you to continue your romance. It is the simple things that will keep your love moving.

MOTHERHOOD AND INTIMACY

I believe many couples lose interest in each other because they do not take time to respect and speak to each other to find out new likings, new interests, and new challenges. Both social and physical intimacies are very important within a marriage. When my kids were young, we had difficulty getting out for dates because of the number of children we had. We had too many children to drop off at one babysitting site. No one wanted to take more than three at a time. So we had to split up our children into three bunches and leave them at the homes of two to three extended family members or friends. These were speedy dates as we were only able to do one thing, such as go to dinner or see a movie. We could not do both because by the time we dropped everyone at their babysitting locations, it was almost time to pick everyone up again. As short as our dates were, however, it was refreshing and emotionally healing to take time away from the kids. They needed time away from us too so they would appreciate us more when we returned.

It is very important that you give each other quality time and attention. Nothing or no one should be more important to you than your spouse at that time. If you feel your marriage or relationship is important and you want it to stay interesting, then you need to put into the marriage what you want to receive from it. Physical intimacy is even more important. If you do not recognize this, then your marriage is over. You must consider your mate's affection and need for physical attention as a priority. Know your mate's sexual rhythm and interests. One may have more of a sex drive, while the other may need more stimulation. Do not take your mate for granted.

When your babies are under the age of two, you may feel exhausted and your spouse may feel a lack of attention. There may even be resentment of the baby as you drag into bed too tired to do anything. If your partner feels neglected, that leaves room for others outside of the home to entice and tempt. Today, couples are in competition with ample access to sexual content on the internet, TV, movies, and even on their own cell phones. The concept of morality in our society has changed, and what was taboo just a few decades ago is readily seen and heard on TV and radio. This common exposure to sexual content can make a monogamous spouse feel there might be something missing, especially as they reach mid-life.

Curiosity and easy access may cause anyone to roam or want to experiment. Communication at this time is crucial to let your spouse know you love them. Mid-day hugs, a quick massage when you sit down, or a love call out of the blue will let your spouse know you love them and that your love *exceeds* any exhaustion. When you do get some time, keep the lovemaking interesting by wearing pretty things and perfume to bed. Find new places to make love or get away for a weekend every once in a while.

During your intimate time together, do not have your mind on other things. Tomorrow's events and problems can wait. Focus on your spouse and make the moment complete. Don't be selfish. Keep your partner in mind during this special moment. This will enhance your love and companionship.

Let him know what pleases you as well. The bedroom is a two-way street and it should not be a 200-yard dash for one if the other prefers a long distance race. Just talk to each other in order to understand each other's needs and timing. The quality of making love will increase if you keep it as a priority.

Furthermore, you should always attempt to avoid unnecessary input from friends. Discussion of other friends' love lives is probably filled with tall tales of stretched-out fantasies that make you wonder or envy. Remember, things may seem better from afar, but if your friend is intimately going from one person to another, then it means they are desiring affection and may need a lot of attention. In addition, discussing your private time with friends could lead to gossip outside your circle of confidentiality. So do not compare your intimate times to others. It is between you and your spouse and is no one else's business. The grass is always greener on the other side until you realize that the other grass has weeds in it, too. So water your own grass, pluck out the weeds, throw some fertilizer on it, and keep it growing.

Most of my acquaintances who have broken up after a long-term marriage suffered from a lack of attention and intimacy. I have found over the years that within our own marriage, our love life has continuously improved because we take time with each other, and we make an effort to expound on the things we each like. An adult movie or magazine once in a while may make you happy, but love is the most important ingredient in sharing a passionate evening together.

Lastly, make the bedroom a special place. Invest time and a little money to decorate your bedroom. Get ideas from design magazines, but at the very least, keep your bedroom clean and treat it as a sanctuary for the both of you. By keeping your bedroom clean, you also teach your children to respect their own belongings and room. If possible, you should avoid doing work in your bed; instead, use your bedroom solely for the pleasurable things in your life.

LET YOUR MATE KNOW YOUR DREAMS

You have your dreams and he may have his own, but you should share at least one dream together. For us it was working on our business, and when that fell through after the recession, bedtime was our time to counsel and console. Our plan now is to buy real estate to support our retirement years. Our plans may have changed, but the direction has always been positive. I enjoy staying in bed and cuddling with my husband while we talk and catch up on each other's lives. Spending time talking about dreams and hopes and planning to make those dreams happen is so important. Ask each other for advice. Share your opinions, but most importantly, listen to each other. Find some common ground and learn something new. I love talking to my husband about our dreams; it gives me hope and makes life a more positive experience.

Fred and me.

Chapter 14

Graduation Day

The best days of my life were the days when my children graduated from high school and, especially, from college. I cannot remember each day in detail, but I do remember at least something from each day. At each event, I was so proud as my child came up the aisle as the song "Pomp and Circumstance" played. I love that song because it signifies victory and that someone has finally made it. Either sung or played, it always makes me cry. It signifies a sense of accomplishment for a great deal of work, a person's refusal to quit in the face of many obstacles. When hearing the song or when I hear the song, I always think of the many who did not make it because of unforeseen circumstances.

There are so many things that can throw you off course. For some, graduation, whether with a four-year degree, post-graduate degree, or even a trade school certificate, is a microcosm of their entire life. The race to classes, handling school, personal schedules, and completing projects is difficult for everyone, but possible. My kids had both experiences. Their foundation at home, tennis, and social nurturing gave them the confidence to pursue their interests and dreams and make their lives productive. That is why it is so important to help them achieve short-term goals early in life.

As Mom, you must have great expectations for them. Push them to achieve and do not settle for mediocre grades due to their situation, school, or friends. Teach them to look above their situation and stay on a path that increases their odds for success. My experiences did not compare to that of my children, who grew up in Los Angeles. I worried about them traveling, dating, and driving, But their experiences are what made them the persons they have become. You do not want to raise a quitter, so train your children to be strong. They need to understand how to say yes to their challenges by getting up every day with an attitude of perseverance.

That is why I love graduation day, because although there are many battles along the way, the general momentum will bring you closer to your goal. I was forty-seven years old when I earned my master's degree. There were classes I had to repeat, tests I failed by two points, and endless projects, but I put one foot in front of the other, and I did it. When I walked across the stage, I was not the youngest, but I certainly wasn't the oldest. I did not think about myself; rather, I thought about my children and how my degree would help our family. But more than that, I wanted them to see that if their mom could do it, then so could they. The hooting and hollering as they called my name was a wonderful and surreal moment.

Your achievements can never be taken from you. You will look back on those experiences to motivate you throughout your life.

Mothers are the Most Incredible People

Remember that, as a mom, you are beautiful and your children are a gift from God. Take care of them and they will make you proud. Love them and enjoy this time of your life. Home is the foundation of life and, as parents, we become witness to children saying, "We made it!" Every parent needs to encourage their child by developing a foundation for them, helping to steer them in the right direction as they transition from year to year. In addition it is important that you take care of yourself and accomplish your own goals too. If you do this with a balance of care, love, and discipline, you will enjoy your children, and their accomplishments will become your own. Then your race will be won.

> *May He grant your heart's desires and make all your*
> *plans succeed.*
> *May we shout for joy when we hear of your victory*
> *and I raise a victory banner. And may the Lord*
> *always answer your prayers.*
>
> ~Psalms 20: 4-6

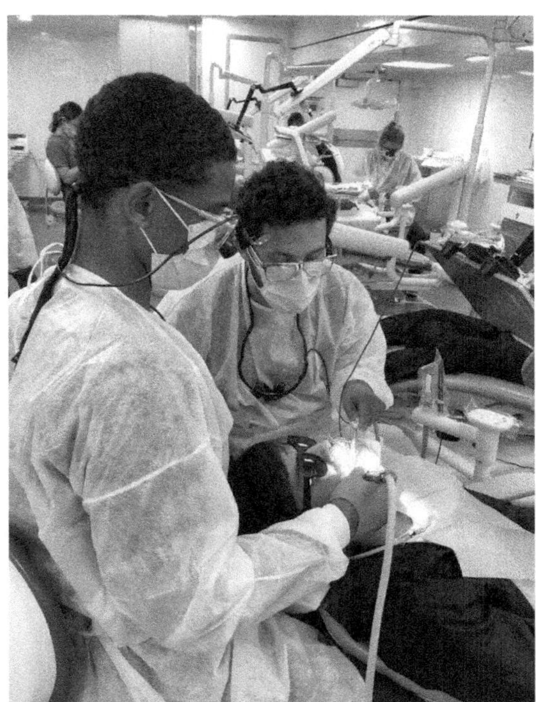

Matthew practicing dentistry.

www.ingramcontent.com/pod-product-compliance
Lightning Source LLC
Chambersburg PA
CBHW070803160726
48004CB00001B/299